CW01336210

# The Wit & Wisdom of
# KERRY

# The Wit & Wisdom of
# KERRY

## BREDA JOY

MERCIER PRESS
IRISH PUBLISHER – IRISH STORY

**MERCIER PRESS**
Cork
www.mercierpress.ie

© Breda Joy, 2015

ISBN: 978 1 78117 337 4

10 9 8 7 6 5 4 3 2 1

A CIP record for this title is available from the British Library

This book is sold subject to the condition that it shall not, by way of trade or otherwise, be lent, resold, hired out or otherwise circulated without the publisher's prior consent in any form of binding or cover other than that in which it is published and without a similar condition including this condition being imposed on the subsequent purchaser.

No part of this publication may be reproduced or transmitted in any form or by any means, electronic or mechanical, including photocopying, recording or any information or retrieval system, without the prior permission of the publisher in writing.

Printed and bound in the EU.

# CONTENTS

| | |
|---|---:|
| Acknowledgements | 9 |
| Introduction | 13 |
| The Spell of Kerry | 19 |
| The Saving Grace of Humour | 28 |
| The Body Politic | 47 |
| A Kerry Character: Jackie Healy-Rae | 74 |
| A Sense of Place | 84 |
| Sporting Days | 97 |
| The Demon Drink | 123 |
| Christmas | 135 |
| A Way with Words | 142 |
| Sex, Marriage and other Shenanigans | 155 |
| Amongst Women | 177 |
| Home Thoughts from Abroad | 194 |
| Words of Wisdom | 212 |
| Famine | 229 |
| Prayers, Blessings, Curses | 238 |
| Schooling | 241 |
| Bibliography | 248 |

*For my aunt,
Lily O'Shaughnessy,
the essence of kindness*

# ACKNOWLEDGEMENTS

I begin by thanking Mary Feehan at Mercier Press for enlisting me to compile this book of quotes and extracts when my earlier work, *Hidden Kerry: the Keys to the Kingdom*, was still taking form in the printing house. To have a book published by such an established house is a great honour and one that I appreciate very much.

The book you are now resting your eyes on has largely come about through extensive reading rather than taking to the highways and byways as I had done to produce my first offering for Mercier. While I cast my own net widely to trawl through the written word pertaining to Kerry, I needed assistance with some of the more specialised subject matter. I sent up a 'flare' for assistance to a number of well-placed friends, acquaintances and, indeed, some total strangers, whose generosity has lent the book a greater breadth and interest.

Special thanks are due in particular to *Kerry's Eye* sports columnist and author Jimmy Darcy, to John O'Mahony of *Killarney Today*, and to Radio Kerry presenter and author Weeshie Fogarty for their contributions. Dr Fiona Brennan's knowledge of playwrights George Fitzmaurice and Pauline Maguire was of immense help, as was her guidance in my quest to include as many women as possible in the work. She also alerted me to John Millington Synge's writings on Kerry.

Historian Dr Kieran Foley, who has written extensively on the Famine, generously shared material relevant to Kerry.

While I was working on the book, the indomitable Jackie Healy-Rae of Kilgarvan passed away. I rank the former TD among the most colourful and inventive practitioners of the spoken word in Kerry, a view that was reinforced as his voice boomed back to me through pages of newsprint and books.

Most of my reading was done in Killarney Library where librarian Éamon Browne and his staff, Kathleen Rice, Noreen Dennehy, Hazel Joy and John McCarthy, are always helpful and welcoming. Libraries are an under-appreciated pillar of our social fabric. Long may they continue to enrich our local communities.

In my work as a journalist, I generally advise people to avoid lists of thanks because they are bound to leave someone out, so it is with some trepidation that I attempt to list additional people who have been of assistance to me but here goes: thanks to historian and author Ryle Dwyer; Cara Trant, manager of The Seanchaí – Kerry Writers' Museum; Micheál de Mórdha, Bainisteoir Ionad an Bhlascaoid; Kerry Travellers' Development Project; Radio Kerry journalist and author Owen O'Shea; the Kennelly family of *Kerry's Eye*; journalists Bridget McAuliffe and Gordon Revington; John Reidy of the *Maine Valley Post*; and to everyone who shared quotes or sent me in fruitful directions.

I owe a debt of gratitude to past and present journalists with *Kerry's Eye*, *The Kerryman* and *The Kingdom*, because these papers are a virtual Aladdin's cave for any researcher. Also, *The Irish Herald* website, Herald.ie, has done the reading public a great service by putting a vast collection of Con Houlihan's columns online.

Finally I would like to thank everyone at my publishers, Mercier Press, especially Wendy Logue, as well as proof-reader Bobby Francis, for their invaluable work on the book.

Here, I have simply been the 'magpie', flitting far and wide in pursuit of the glitter that caught my eye. It has been a privilege to draw into the light shards of the best of so many writers and speakers born of Kerry and associated with Kerry. Mine is the prism, theirs is the light.

# INTRODUCTION

'One wonders in these places why anyone is left in Dublin, or London, or Paris, when it would be better, one would think, to live in a tent or hut with this magnificent sea and sky, and to breathe this wonderful air, which is like wine in one's teeth.' Learning that this quote from John Millington Synge referred to West Kerry and not, as I had presumed for years, the Aran Islands, was one of the discoveries I made while researching this book. Synge's lyrical description belongs to a rich bank of descriptive writing inspired down through the years by the extraordinary Kerry landscape, but if beauty doesn't boil the pot, it won't shift this book either.

The opening quote is just one element of the kaleidoscope I have assembled to touch on as many elements as possible of the nuanced life of Kerry. For instance, another gem of a different variety comes from Sigerson Clifford, the Cahersiveen writer, who, I hold, could equal Synge in the poetry of his language but chose to go the way of hilarity when writing his own funeral instructions. Here's a wee taster: 'Soon as the coffin arrives pop me in, screw down the lid and tell those who want to stare at me to shove off.' The full reference is filed under 'The Saving Grace of Humour'.

Selecting the quotations has been a tightrope act in the sense that I have had to balance competing demands to maintain the common touch while also doing justice to weightier utterances. In short, I had to meet the expectations of a book peppered with throwaway lines associated with the cute Kerry man or woman, but I also had to represent a county which has produced leading national figures, such as 'the Liberator' Daniel O'Connell, and has been at the centre of numerous critical news-making events in Irish life.

Always in the mind of the Kerry person communicating an understanding of the kingdom is a keen awareness of the stereotypes that people trade in outside its boundaries. Take note that there's a lot more to us than ye think, as was well expressed by Kerry Bishop Kevin McNamara in an interview given just after he was appointed Archbishop of Dublin in 1984: 'It would be wrong to give the impression that I am moving from a rural backwater, with no cultural life or exchange of ideas, to a completely different place.' (Indulge me for a moment while I give a little of the back story to that quote. I was a fledgling freelance journalist trying to eke out a crust when the cleric gave me that interview, which was published in *The Sunday Press*. My clearest recollection is that he used the phrase 'aboriginal backwater' which had a great ring to it, but when I resurrected the actual newspaper clipping, the word 'rural' was there in front of me. I like to think that a sub-editor simplified the text, but I will never know.)

But enough of my Kerry neuroses for now. It is the stock-in-trade of my profession as a journalist to inform and entertain: this book is weighted to reflect that duality. While there is a core of significant quotes that would have been common to any researcher, the circles radiating out from there reflect my personal interests and approach, which have been previously described as 'idiosyncratic' and 'unorthodox'. In other words, folks, you are getting a very mixed bag. No doubt there will be some omissions and I put my hands up in advance on that score. (I must note here that, in the interests of inclusivity, I did contact two centres for asylum seekers in Killarney and Tralee, but their experiences of life in Kerry have yet to be committed to print.)

The book is divided into a variety of sections such as politics, sport, alcohol, marriage, humour and wisdom; it journeys from the sublime to the ridiculous, stopping off at assorted stations in between. Emigration was a section that was very important to me, because the overseas 'constituency' is too often overlooked, a view you will find powerfully expressed by some of the emigrants quoted here. However, this is a largely 'historic' view of emigration given the advent of social media and cheaper air travel which, to a large extent, have diluted the separation and finality, with the one notable exception of the undocumented Irish in the United States.

I read as widely as I could, ranging from well-known Kerry writers – the 'usual suspects' – to memoirs, journals and anthologies below the general radar. As I have stated in the acknowledgements, newspaper reports of past decades provided rich pickings and proved to me that news is not as ephemeral as I believed in the days when I wrapped heads of cabbage and boxes of Zip firelighters in yesterday's pages behind the counter of our family grocery shop.

As always, the beauty of taking on a challenge like this is the discovery of new material and the rediscovery of 'old friends'. The Castleisland colossus Con Houlihan is one of my own favourites, and I regularly return to his work as a matter of course (I have a much-cherished copy of *Windfalls* that he signed for me at his Portobello home). The inclusion of so many examples of his extraordinary wit and command of the English language will come as no surprise to his fans. But a name possibly less familiar to many is that of the Listowel wordsmith Seán McCarthy. Reading through some of his columns in *The Kerryman* of the 1990s, I felt that a revival of his general work is long overdue. Another writer who has lapsed into obscurity in Kerry, apart from in her native Cahersiveen, is the playwright Pauline Maguire, who I am pleased to include. Rory O'Connor's *Gander at the Gate* is a memoir I would highly recommend for its wonderful anecdotes and style of writing, evidence of which you will find in short extracts quoted here. For further examples of remarkable storytelling and writing, dip into *Bibeanna: Memories from a Corner of Ireland* and *The Iveragh Peninsula: A Cultural Atlas of the Ring of Kerry*, two treasures I discovered on the shelves of Killarney Library.

The theory that there are six degrees of separation in the world shrinks to three degrees when it comes to Ireland. From time immemorial Kerry itself has an uncanny knack of making universal connections. Within these pages you will find a connection between Kilgarvan and Martin Luther King Jnr, Dingle and Dolly Parton, Killarney and Brendan Behan. Even the handsome Hollywood heartthrob George Clooney gets a few words in. However does he? Turn the page and away with you.

# THE SPELL OF KERRY

To be born in Kerry is an accident of birth over which one has no control. To then decide to live in the county is a conscious decision that makes a person a Kingdomite.

The rest of those born here, but who settle elsewhere are spiritual Kerry persons …

The third group consists of Kerry persons by adoption. That status is conferred on those who are born elsewhere, but who become ensnared by Kerry and all it means …

All three strands of Kerry people should each day chant the mantra 'A day out of Kerry is a day wasted.'

*(Padraig Kennelly in Valerie O'Sullivan's* I am of Kerry*)*

Being born a Kerryman, in my opinion, is the greatest gift that God can bestow on any man. When you belong to Kerry, you know you have a head start on the other fellow … In belonging to Kerry, you belong to the elements. You belong to the spheres spinning in the heavens.

*(John B. Keane in Jimmy Woulfe's* Voices of Kerry*)*

Sometimes the media give the impression that people in Dublin are completely different from people in Kerry. Whereas in Kerry you have a whole cross-section – country, and very sophisticated and highly educated people.

It would be wrong to give the impression that I am moving from a rural backwater, with no cultural life or exchange of ideas, to a completely different place. Kerry is a place which has an extremely varied social and cultural life and I owe a lot to my eight years here from so many different points of view.

*(Bishop Kevin McNamara of Kerry in an interview in* The Sunday Press, *25 November 1984, after the announcement of his appointment as Archbishop of Dublin)*


Kerry was my father's inspiration, a country of magic. But I could tell he was haunted by it too. It was the place where he had known uncomplicated happiness, but it was also the source of much of his pain.

*(Fergal Keane writing about his father, Éamon, in* All of These People*)*


I feel spiritually much more released and much more at peace with nature in Kerry. I know Kerry people are rogues. I'm a rogue myself. Its beauty is physical and spiritual. There is an atmosphere and serenity in Kerry which you will not find any place else.

*(Dermot Kinlen referring to his time as a barrister, in Jimmy Woulfe's* Voices of Kerry*)*

Up Kerry, Up Us.

> *(Salutation of Padraig Kennelly at social gatherings)*

Sweet Muckross must I leave you?

> *(A member of the Herbert family, source unknown)*

It will be the greatest playground in the world, for there is not another like it and I know them all.

> *(Senator Arthur Vincent on presenting the Muckross Estate, with his parents-in-law William and Agnes Bowers Bourn, to the Irish State in 1932 in memory of his late wife, Maud. The Bourn Vincent Memorial Park became the nucleus of Killarney National Park)*

The air is soft, the water is soft – in Kerry. I recently met at a meeting of the Irish Genealogical Research Society, a man who told me he went over to Kerry to have a bath in the soft water! The voices of the people are soft – to sum up, the climate is soft.

> *(Bertha Beatty,* Kerry Memories*)*

Many an old woman in Ireland had a nicer place and more pleasant place to study than this, but I prefer this lonely place to any other place in Ireland. The golden mountains of Ireland are without mist before me. The sea is pouring itself against the rocks and running up in dark ravines and caves where the seals live. We are not disturbed by the uproar and noise of the city. There is a fine hedge around us and we are inside the Summerhouse of Peace.

*(Peig Sayers,* An Old Woman's Reflections*)*


Or, were you with me amidst the Alpine scenery that surrounds my humble abode, listening to the eternal roar of the mountain torrent, as it bounds through the rocky defiles of my native glens, I would venture to tell you how I was born within the sound of the everlasting wave …

*(William J. Daunt quoting Daniel O'Connell in* Personal Reflections of the Late Daniel O'Connell, MP*)*


I was born in Gleann Loic, under the shadow of Mount Eagle, on the last day of January 1931. At sunrise, my mother told me. Sunrise is late in Dún Chaoin, because of the bulk of the mountain to the east of us. But we have long, wonderful sunsets above the islands and the sea.

*(Siobhán a' Chró, Bean Uí Dhubháin, in Brenda Ní Shúilleabháin's* Bibeanna: Memories from a Corner of Ireland*)*

## The Spell of Kerry

I am a boy who was born and bred in the Great Blasket, a small, truly Gaelic island which lies north-west of the coast of Kerry, where the storms of the sky and the wild sea beat without ceasing from end to end of the year and from generation to generation against the wrinkled rocks which stand above the waves and wash in and out of the coves where the seals make their homes ...

I took a car to Dunquin and how my heart opened when I reached Slea Head and saw the Blasket, Inish-na-Bró and Inish-vick-illaun stretched out before me in the sea to the west! I was as gay as a starling as I went down to Dunquin ...

*(Maurice O'Sullivan,* Twenty Years A-Growing*)*


I walked up this morning along the slope from the east to the top of Sybil Head, where one comes out suddenly on the brow of a cliff with a straight fall of many hundred feet into the sea. It is a place of indescribable grandeur, where one can see Carrantuohill and the Skelligs and Loop Head and the full sweep of the Atlantic, and, over all, the wonderfully tender and searching light that is only seen in Kerry. Looking down the drop of five or six hundred feet, the height is so great that the gannets flying close over the sea look like white butterflies, and the choughs like flies fluttering behind them.

*(J. M. Synge,* John M. Synge in West Kerry*)*

There was a very important battle just outside Kilgarvan, which stopped the Normans getting into South Kerry. And today you can see the Normans in North Kerry and the Celts in South Kerry …

*(Dermot Kinlen in Jimmy Woulfe's* Voices of Kerry*)*

The whole sight of wild islands and sea was as clear and cold and brilliant as what one sees in a dream with the singularly severe glory that is in the character of this place.

*(J. M. Synge,* John M. Synge in West Kerry*)*

All those years that I had felt sorry for my grandparents because they were old and poor and lived in a little house with no electricity or running water and they never went anywhere except to church or to the neighbours or, for my grandfather, to the pub. All those years and I had never realised that they were rich beyond most people's dreams, for they had peace. When I sat and looked at the mountains, I could have it too …

As I sat there, I realised my grandparents had given me an inheritance which was treasure beyond a price. They had given me back my mountains and my mountains would give me peace.

*(Maureen Erde,* Help! I'm an Irish Innkeeper*)*

In remembering past times, I remember most my husband's strong love for his native place. Every year as July edged nearer August he became restless. As evening came on he was out in the back garden, carefully examining the night sky for signs of good weather. Then one night he would say, 'I'll be off so in the morning' and thus the annual visit to Cahirciveen, County Kerry, would begin. Like the scholar-gypsy, rumoured sightings of him came back to us … But the visit to Cahirciveen lasted at most three to four days and he was back to us again, smiling and at peace with the world, like a pilgrim returning from a holy place, and content to remain in his Dublin back garden for the rest of the summer. In January 1985, on a day of snow and ice, we took him back to Cahirciveen for the last time.

*(Marie Clifford, preface to* Irish Short Stories *by her husband, Sigerson Clifford)*


Some believe that a landscape explains a people, defines them. I don't know. But I *do* know that landscape influences people – who can not but be influenced by breakers in a gale charging the cliffs in Clochar or Ballybunion; who can not but be pared down to bare essentials by the mountains of Corca Dhuibhne or Uíbh Ráthach; who can not but be awed by a stippled sunset over Cnoc an Fhómhair or a silver moon tinselling a bog in Sliabh Luachra or Oidhreacht Uí Chonchubhair?

*(Gabriel Fitzmaurice,* Kerry Through Its Writers*)*

One day alone in Kerry, away from the roads on mountains that go down sharply to the sea and you understand why in lonely places the Irish believe in fairies and things not of this earth …

As the road goes on into Kerry I come across stretches of country from which melancholy seems to ooze from the hard soil. There is a sadness and a disillusion in the air. The very rain weeps rather than falls over the land and the wind is a sigh.

*(H.V. Morton*, In Search of Ireland)

I'm living in the mouth of Valentia Harbour. Leac a 'Bhealaigh is on the Beginish side. When you see the swells breaking over that, it's an ever-changing scene, and the Blaskets and the Tiaracht in the background.

And the Dingle Peninsula over to the right. And the Iveragh Mountains heading out to the other side … It's something I am very much at peace with.

*(Mick O'Connell quoted in 'Mick O'Connell: A Football Legend',*
The Kerryman, *18 February 2000)*

We are five and a half miles from the centre of Killarney, up in the hills, up under Mangerton Mountain. It's the parish of Coolies. There is a posh part of Muckross and there is a part of it that is in the commonage, like, and we are in the wilderness part of it. You are looking straight out at the Reeks, the Tomies and

## THE SPELL OF KERRY

behind them is the Gap of Dunloe. And then you are looking at Torc Mountain with the mist down on it today a little bit. You have the Punch Bowl and behind me is the Horses Glen and Stoompa and all the way over to East Kerry you have Cappagh and in the far distance the Paps of Dana. We are surrounded by mountains here and you have all the furze and the bracken and the dwarf furze growing around the house. Up here in the nights we hear the stags bellowing because the rut is on. It's magical.

*(John Moriarty quoted by Weeshie Fogarty on* Weeshie's Week, Radio Kerry, *5 June 2007)*


It would be nice to wax lyrical about Kerry and about being from Kerry. To catch from an office stool the wasp-yellow fields where the kelp streamers lie, like Sigerson Clifford …

For all its beauty, this is a county of men. It is a county that favours male games, male committees, mostly male juries, where football is a 'religion'. … It is a county where you could imagine a second run at The Kerry Babies, a county where to lie and to deceive are far more acceptable than in most. And it's not all codding.

It's a county which has begun believing its own tourism marketing 'myths' – not alas the ones of Deirdre keening Naoise in the cave near Rossbeigh, but newer, emptier ones of perfection, and which reacts with fury once those myths are challenged.

*(Anne Lucey in Valerie O'Sullivan's* I am of Kerry*)*

# THE SAVING GRACE OF HUMOUR

When the next jobber came around he asked my father, 'Are you selling the pig?'

'No,' my father said, 'I am taking him to Ballybunion on his holidays.'

*(Éamon Kelly,* The Apprentice*)*

There wasn't as much lean in them as you'd draw with a solitary stroke of a red biro.

*(John B. Keane on a Kerryman describing fat rashers. 'Kerry', in Gabriel Fitzmaurice's* Kerry Through Its Writers*)*

She's a great girl – you couldn't draw Vim to her.

*(A Castleisland man's description of his daughter-in-law. 'Sheila Prendiville's',* The Kerryman, *21 October 2004)*

I hear that some people believe that not drinking or smoking can prolong their lives. Well in that case they have only got themselves to blame.

*(Moss Keane,* Rucks, Mauls & Gaelic Football*)*

I have always described the Kerryman as the greater, hard-necked, atlantical warbler, otherwise known as the Kerryman. He quests individually, and in flocks, for all forms of diversion and is to be found high and low, winter and summer, wherever there is the remotest prospect of drink, sex, confusion or commotion.

*(John B. Keane's definition of a Kerryman, in Jimmy Woulfe's* Voices of Kerry*)*

But he wrote beautiful things about the Greenville team and all the teams he'd be in and everything, and I had beautiful bags for putting the tea into and he used to write them on the bags and they were gorgeous tea bags. 'Jesus, John,' I'd say, 'you'll destroy my tea bags.'

*(Mary Keane [wife of John B.] in conversation with Gabriel Fitzmaurice,* Cork Literary Review, Volume XV, *2013)*

At the time of which I write, the Lartigue railway from Listowel connected Ballybunion with the world ... Stories were numerous of the difficulty in balancing the carriages, and one was that a very fat woman once took her seat on one side of the carriage. No one could be found to make the weight correct on the other side, so a cow was put on board. This is one of, it is said, 10,000 jokes about the Lartigue.

*(Bertha Beatty,* Kerry Memories*)*

What spelling have you, only write it down.

> *(A Kerry hurling selector in the 1960s to a sports reporter, quoted fondly in* The Kerryman *newsroom in Clash, Tralee, for many years afterwards)*

We don't have headaches in Caherdaniel.

> *(Postmistress Maura Moriarty's response to the request of a visitor for paracetamol. Maura, who died in 2014, was almost a one-woman Bord Fáilte for her parish. Quoted by Michael Corridan in 'Remembering Maura Moriarty',* Caherdaniel Parish Magazine, *2015)*

If you're seeking the source of humming which is musically expressive and linguistically effective ask one of your relatives for the loan of a substantial sum of money.

> *(John B. Keane,* The Little Book of John B. Keane)

I wouldn't know what Facebook was if it came in the door.

> *(Judge James O'Connor,* The Kerryman, *7 January 2015)*

The elderly fan wrote: 'I liked your book Seán. What I liked most about it was your photo on the cover. Your "lived-in" face – lined and creased like an unmade bed.'

> *(Seán McCarthy,* The Kerryman, *5 January 1990)*

I phoned Mary, newly divorced, and told her the news. She called me a moron for being banged by a bishop.

*(Annie Murphy on her relationship with Bishop Eamonn Casey, in* Forbidden Fruit*)*


John Kenny told them in Rathkeale I was the leading authority in Ireland on drains. I brought my wellington boots everywhere after that. I had never done a case on drains until John Kenny gave me one, which I won in Rathkeale. He put out the word that I was the man on drains.

*(Dermot Kinlen in Jimmy Woulfe's* Voices of Kerry*)*


The doctors in Trallock wouldn't know their balls from their tonsils.

*(John B. Keane,* The Little Book of John B. Keane)


I missed Italia '90, I was in Italy at the time.

*(Con Houlihan, quoted by Eanna Brophy in* The Sunday Times, *3 June 2012)*


Poetry is bad enough without it being long.

*(John Faulkner to John B. Keane, as recounted to me by Gabriel Fitzmaurice in 2014)*

'I want them to gossip about me,' she told me. 'It keeps them happy. I bought a new bed last week, and my neighbours wanted to know was it a double or a single. I told them it takes three.'

*(Lily van Oost in Breda Joy's* Hidden Kerry*)*


A steamroller passed through the village last week.

*(A single, solitary news item published in the 'North Kerry notes' of* The Kerryman *some time in the 1980s and displayed on the office wall in Clash, Tralee, for many years)*


He had a crease in his trousers that'd shave a gooseberry for you, and the tie he had around his neck I wouldn't like any bull to see it.

*(Éamon Kelly,* The Apprentice*)*


A certain roystering gentleman named Jack Ray got drunk and fell asleep in the woods of Kilcoleman. Some of the Godfrey boys, seeing him prostrate and with foam on his lips, ran to summon their father, saying to him: 'There's a man dead in the wood.'

Sir William hastened to the spot, and having put on his glasses to get a view of the corpse, observed: 'Come away, my boys, this man dies once a week.'

*(Samuel Hussey,* The Reminiscences of an Irish Land Agent*)*

'Gi'me more mate!' says he.

'You've enough,' she told him. 'If you ate any more of it the bull'll be roaring inside you.'

'Why then,' says he, 'it won't be for the want of turnips.'

*(Éamon Kelly,* The Apprentice*)*


One lad below there said no one will eat a bite of her – she's as yellow as a sovereign.

*(Jerome O'Leary, owner of the long-lived cow, Big Bertha, on the findings of a laboratory test in Cork. Breda Joy,* Hidden Kerry*)*


Quare times said the cat as the clock fell on it.

*(Éamon Kelly,* Ireland's Master Storyteller: The Collected Stories of Éamon Kelly*)*


I was hoping it had the sweat still in it. I'm honoured, thank you very much. Stick it on (laughs).

*(Dolly Parton to Páidí Ó Sé after he presented her with his Kerry jersey at his bar in Ventry,* YouTube, *27 November 2012)*


Welcome to Dinglewood.

*(Dolly Parton in Páidí Ó Sé's pub in Dingle,* YouTube, *27 November 2012)*

No Bus/Coach tours or loud Americans. Thank you.

*(Sign posted on the window of Peter's Place, a Waterville hostel and café, in 2014. The notice fanned a media storm internationally, as locals feared repercussions for the tourist trade and Americans took umbrage.*
Irish Independent, *21 July 2014)*


He has the same chance as a three-legged hare at a coursing meeting.

*(John B. Keane,* The Little Book of John B. Keane*)*


Mary Hold the Candle til I Shave the Gander's Leg.

*(Name of a tune, as given in Maidhc Dainín Ó Sé's* House Don't Fall on Me*)*


The question of using one of the car parks for coaches is commendable but will not please all the drivers – some of whom would wish to take their vehicles to bed with them.

*(Superintendent Michael Burke in a letter to Killarney Town Council,* The Kerryman, *date unknown)*


There's enough lies written on the headstones of Ireland without my adding to them.

*(Maggie in John B. Keane's* Big Maggie*)*

I would like to thank Michael Fassbender for taking over the frontal nude responsibility that I had. Really Michael, honestly, you can play golf like this with your hands behind your back (mocking a golf swing with his hands behind back). Go for it man, do it!

*(George Clooney jokes with the Killarney actor who was co-nominee with him for the Best Actor in a Motion Picture Drama at the Golden Globes 2012. Fassbender was nominated for his role in* Shame. www.huffingtonpost.com, *1 June 2012)*


John B. only puts down what we say, and then charges us to hear it ourselves.

*(A Listowel friend of the playwright)*


I tend to cook anything that might not burn.

*(Canon Brian Lougheed,* The Kerryman, *27 November 1998)*


I can get television stations from all over the world, from America, Australia, France, Switzerland, everywhere – but I'd swop the lot of them to be able to watch *Glenroe*.

*(Eileen Cronin, who used satellite TV to get reception in her home at the foot of Carrauntuohill,* The Kerryman, *2 February 1990)*

I'd have made a lovely priest – full of compassion and altar wine.

*(Moss Keane,* Rucks, Mauls & Gaelic Football*)*

''Tis all doom and gloom today, Seáneen, and when it isn't, it's all this talk about trouble and sex.'

'But Katie,' I said, to keep the craic going, 'there was no shortage of sex in your young day either. Not with ten children!'

There was a flash of laughter in the green eyes then, as she said, 'Will you whish. In my day it was more like attack and defend, and I didn't defend too well.'

*(Seán McCarthy,* 'McCarthy's Women'*,* The Kerryman, *6 July 1990)*

The veracity of an Irishman is never considerable, for as a rule he will say what he thinks is likely to please you rather than state any unpleasant fact.

*(Samuel Hussey,* The Reminiscences of an Irish Land Agent*)*

The propagation of bingo is the ultimate role of the Catholic Church in Ireland.

*(John B. Keane,* The Little Book of John B. Keane*)*

I read with considerable mystification the other day where Cardinal Tomás Ó Fiaich claimed that RTÉ's *Glenroe* programme was giving St Bridget a bad name and that parents were refusing to call their female offspring after the saint because of the character, Biddy, depicted in the programme.

Now with all due respect to the good cardinal, I think the man is talking rubbish ...

Let us consider the facts. Biddy is the hardy low-set sturdy ball of a woman who spends the entire programme sloping around the farmyard carrying buckets, bales, and four stone bags of spuds in an entirely admirable display of industry. You rarely see the woman unless she is almost hidden underneath a mighty load of something or other.

*(Mickey McConnell, 'Biddy from Glenroe: an inspiration to us all',*
The Kerryman, *9 February 1990)*

But how does one recognise a typical wind-breaker? What are his classical points? ... Your true, sneak-wind-breaker sits immobile and expressionless. There is never the slightest hint that he is the responsible party. Look for a man whose expression would suggest that wind-breaking is the last thought in his head and avoid him like you would a plague, for deep under that seemingly innocent exterior is the potential for a thousand outbursts, long, short and medium.

*(John B. Keane, 'Breaking Wind', in*
Unlawful Sex and Other Testy Matters*)*

Éamon Kelly gave me great advice – he said you're nowhere without a good woman to your back, and then added – but that's not where you want her ...

*(Michael Colgan,* The Kerryman, *19 November 1999)*


Father Ferris' views of the world were so unorthodox that in ecclesiastical circles the term 'feresy' was coined to cover his many sub-heretical opinions ...

He invented a new world, 'pollantory', a place where souls went to have good knocked out of them before they went to hell, just as they went to purgatory to have the bad knocked out of them before they went to heaven.

*(Fintan O'Toole, referring to Asdee parish priest, Fr William Ferris. 'Seeing is Believing', in Gabriel Fitzmaurice's* The Kerry Anthology*)*


It's a load of codswallop. There is no question of anyone luring Fungi away from Dingle ...

This talk of kidnapping is a kind of dangerous thing to be saying.

They must have been very short of news to print something like that. It's pure sensationalism.

*(Dingle ESB worker John O'Connor, who first found the dolphin, reacts to speculation that attempts were being made to lure the dolphin to Cahersiveen,* The Kerryman, *19 January 1990)*

Brendan Kennelly, who used to come to the dances in Ballybunion, said they always had to give the sergeant's daughters a duty dance in case they were caught without a light on their bikes going home.

*(Mary Cummins, 'The Sergeant', in Gabriel Fitzmaurice's* Kerry Through Its Writers)

My father, Peter Bodkin Hussey, was for a long time a barrister at the Irish Bar, practising in the Four Courts, where more untruths are spoken than anywhere else in the three kingdoms, except in the House of Commons during an Irish debate.

*(Samuel Hussey,* The Reminiscences of an Irish Land Agent)

There were these two bachelor brothers who came into possession of a glossy magazine with pages of women dressed in different degrees of apparel.

After some amount of study, the men selected two models, one in her winter best and one, you could say, more fit for bed.

Some weeks passed and one brother enquired, 'When do you think they will be sending on our women?'

"Twon't be long now, I make out,' the other brother replied. 'They're after sending their clothes ahead.'

*(As heard by the author at Scartaglen Rambling House, Monday 10 November 2014)*

Small Daddy came from Ballinskelligs and Irish was his first language, as it was my grandmother's ... English only my father had and that was the language in our house.

'Hard for him to have the Irish,' Small Daddy remarked, 'and his father a foreigner from Caragh Bridge.'

*(Sigerson Clifford, 'My South Kerry Grandfathers',
in* Irish Short Stories*)*

Better-looking men than me such as vets, inseminators, insurance agents, seed salesmen and warble-fly inspectors seem to enjoy immunity, but pull on a postman's uniform and you're a target for every sex-starved damsel in the district.

*(John B. Keane,* The Little Book of John B. Keane*)*

My eldest brother, John, was drowned at St Malo. He was unmarried, and his profession was to do nothing as handsomely as he could.

*(Samuel Hussey,* The Reminiscences of an Irish Land Agent*)*

Don't some people live very far away.

*(Remark of a Portmagee man passing Newbridge on his maiden train voyage to Croke Park. 'Travellers' tales on the track to Dublin',
in Con Houlihan's* Windfalls*)*

'Did you hear the news? I'm after willing my body to science, but one thing sure, they will never find out what went on up here,' Cornie Tangney said, pointing to his head.

*(Cornie quoted by Michael Lenihan at Scartaglen Rambling House)*


There is more sustenance in a bull's eye than there is in a pint of Guinness.

*(A quote of Fr William Ferris related to me by Nancy McAuliffe, Duagh)*


I don't want any costly coffin. If a plain box is good enough for the Pope a middle price coffin is good enough for me. Too good, maybe. Soon as the coffin arrives pop me in, screw down the lid and tell those who want to stare at me to shove off. When they didn't come to admire me when I was worth looking at, I don't want them peering me when I can't see what they're thinking about me.

*(Funeral instructions written by Sigerson Clifford in October 1984 and preserved in Cahersiveen Library)*


Rats were dancing polka sets around the place.

*(Kerry County Councillor Donal Grady warns of a ten-fold increase in rodents because of illegal dumping,* Kerry's Eye, *12 March 2015)*

The car performed up to specification but Clarke did not ... He said if he ran out of petrol he ran it on paraffin oil. He even declared that one day when there was nothing else to be done he ran it on a bottle of whiskey.

*(Rory O'Connor,* Gander at the Gate*)*


She was a big fat woman, although not too tall, and of all the women I ever met, she spent more time looking at herself in mirrors. There were mirrors in every room and two in the hallway, and 'twas no small house, I'll tell you. 'Twas as if she thought that every time she looked into the mirror she might have got a bit better looking ... She was always trying new fads to slim herself down. This diet and that diet, this cream and that cream for morning, noon and night, but she might as well have been rubbing on the spit of a cuckoo.

*(Rory O'Connor,* Gander at the Gate*)*


'It's that damnable rogue of a Daniel O'Connell,
He's now making children in Dublin by steam.'
'Oh, children, aroo,' replied the old woman.
'ainm an diabhal! [by the devil!], is he crazy at last?
Is there sign of a war or a sudden rebellion
Or what is the reason he wants them so fast?'

*(A popular ballad summed up Daniel O'Connell's reputation as the alleged father of countless children born outside of wedlock)*

I'm not a trained mourner … I can't olagón or moan or look for the arm of another hypocrite to support me.

*(Maggie in John B. Keane's* Big Maggie*)*


Because of the tax on tall hats, the normal headgear of that time, Maurice wouldn't pay the tax – as a good smuggler he naturally objected to such extortion – but wore a hunting cap instead.

*(Explanation given by Donal O'Sullivan for the nickname of Daniel O'Connell's uncle, Maurice 'Hunting Cap' O'Connell, in Richard Hayward's* In the Kingdom of Kerry*)*


A wooden leg is like an adopted child. With all the ups and downs in the world it could be better to you than one of your own in the end.

*(John B. Keane, 'Letters of a Matchmaker', in* Celebrated Letters of John B. Keane, *Vol. 1)*


When Kerry absolutely thrashed Dublin in the 1978 All-Ireland football final, a good friend asked Con Houlihan how his partner, Harriet Duffin, a Dub, had taken news of the defeat.

'House private, no flowers,' Con replied in a flash.

*(Con Houlihan's Ireland – The Lost Essays,* Irish Independent, *2 March 2013)*

It would bring tears from a glass eye.

> *(Cork musician Jackie Daly quoting an elderly man's reaction to his rendition of 'The Blue Mount Waltz' at The Gathering Festival, Killarney INEC, 22 February 2015)*

I was the leader of the underground movement there [Castlemartyr boarding school]. We had a new priest and he was a dictator and we decided to make life difficult for him. I was the leader and editor of our paper. It was hand-written, seditious and not altogether polite.

> *(Con Houlihan describing* The College Courier, *which gave him his first editorial experience.* The Kerryman, *19 June 1998)*

Do you know something Coneen … we're like Napoleon's Army on retreat from Moscow.

> *(Fiddler Jerry McCarthy to Con Houlihan as they sheltered from hail under a hawthorn bush. 'Ireland's travelling minstrels – fiddlers on the hoof', in Con Houlihan's* Windfalls*)*

And the priest's whingeing began. I could have put my foot in his mouth but I was wearing stiletto heels and I didn't want to maim him – I just wanted him to shut up.

> *(Maureen Erde,* Help! I'm an Irish Innkeeper*)*

Comaoin ort, arsa an dreoilín, nuair a mhuín sé san fharraige mhór. (You owe me, said the wren, when he pissed in the ocean.)

*(Given to me by Proinsias M. Ó Donnchadha)*


If your mother says she loves you, check it out.

*(A truism imparted to* Kerryman *sports journalist Éamonn Horan, in Clash, Tralee, by a visiting Chicago reporter)*


One of his favourite stories concerned going to the butcher for a pig's head. When asked where the butcher should cut it, Moss quickly answered, 'As close to the arse as you can.'

*(Moss Keane,* Rucks, Mauls & Gaelic Football*)*


Feck your water charges, Enda!!! Cordal, Ireland.

*(Message posted on the giant screen in Times Square, New York, by Padraig Dignan, Cordal, and Michael Walsh, Castleisland, and four other friends, recorded by Michelle Crean in* Kerry's Eye, *23 October 2014)*


There were more people in the GPO than in Tiananmen Square to judge from the number of claimants looking for pensions.

*(Dermot Kinlen in Jimmy Woulfe's* Voices of Kerry*)*

I remember cycling to Ventry one night on an old crock of a bike with only a turnip with the top cut off as a saddle.

*(Bríd Bean Uí Mhaoileoin in Brenda Ní Shúilleabháin's* Bibeanna: Memories from a Corner of Ireland*)*


For fox sake please come in and buy something.

*(This phrase, coined by Katie O'Connell of Killarney, appeared beneath a stuffed fox resting on a chaise longue in the window of her shop at the height of the recession. The humorous image was captured by photographer Valerie O'Sullivan and appeared on the front page of* The Irish Times *on 9 February 2009)*

# THE BODY POLITIC

They are a breed apart.

*(Kerry journalist Katie Hannon, in her book* The Naked Politician*)*


Once you put your name on a ballot paper that's a real statement of your self-worth. I just do not accept any shite over in Leinster House who says he or she is humble. We might all have much to be humble about but we've never found it. The fact is once you put your name on a ballot paper that's an egotistical action. You're saying to people 'vote for me'. And that's egotism writ large.

*(Senator Joe O'Toole from Dingle in Katie Hannon's*
The Naked Politician*)*


When we look down into the fathomless depth of this infamy of the heads of the Fenian conspiracy, we must acknowledge that eternity is not long enough, nor hell hot enough to punish such miscreants.

*(Bishop of Kerry David Moriarty,* The Irish Times,
*19 February 1867)*

Arise, Knocknagoshel, and take your place among the nations of this earth.

> *(Banner carried by Knocknagoshel supporters of Charles Stewart Parnell to a rally on his behalf in Newcastlewest in 1891. The words are recorded on a plaque on a house in the village)*

I believe in the Corporal Works of Mercy, the Ten Commandments, the American Declaration of Independence and James Connolly's outline of a socialist society ... Most of my life I've been called a lunatic because I believe that I am my brother's keeper. I organise poor and exploited workers, I fight for the civil rights of minorities, and I believe in peace. It appears to have become old-fashioned to make social commitments – to want a world free of war, poverty and disease. This is my religion.

> *(Michael J. Quill quoted in 'Martin Luther King, Jnr, and the Man from Kerry'.* Footnotes to Irish History in the Americas, *www.irishamericanfootnotes.blogspot.ie)*

Mike Quill was one of the pioneers of the modern trade union movement who never lost the fighting spirit of the thirties. He was among the giants who lifted our sick nation from despair and poverty by organizing the unorganized and by inaugurating a new era for America, the era of social welfare and social responsibility. The trade union pioneers of the thirties designed the earliest anti-poverty program and called it the trade union movement. They fought to give it an honored place in our society, and today a whole nation benefits from their vision and militancy.

Mike Quill was also a pioneer in race relations. When it was hard and often bruising to stand up for equality, he was tough enough and bold enough to make himself clearly heard … Negroes desperately needed men like Mike Quill who fearlessly said what was true even though it offended. This is why Negroes shall miss Mike Quill.

Mike Quill was a fighter for decent things all his life – Irish independence, labor organization, and racial equality. He spent his life ripping the chains of bondage off his fellow man. When the totality of a man's life is consumed with enriching the lives of others, this is a man the ages will remember – this is a man who has passed on but who has not died.

> *(The tribute paid in 1966 by Martin Luther King Jnr to Michael J. Quill, the Kilgarvan man who emigrated to New York in 1926 and founded the Transport Workers Union of America in 1934. Shirley Quill,* Michael Quill, Himself: A Memoir*)*

Mike Quill is an impossible-ist.

> *(The American poet Carl Sandburg, 1966. Shirley Quill,* Michael Quill, Himself: A Memoir*)*

Thirty years in Dáil Éireann and never opened his mouth except to pick his teeth.

*(John B. Keane,* The Little Book of John B. Keane*)*

I am reminded of what a farmer said recently about a different member of the government. Asking the Taoiseach [Bertie Ahern] a question is like trying to play handball against a haystack. You hear a dull thud and the ball does not come back to you. It goes all over the world, but it certainly does not come back to the person asking the question.

*(Deputy Joe O'Higgins, Leaders' Questions, Dáil Éireann, Leinster House, 29 January 2003, www.oireachtas.ie)*

There is no question but that you could be doing a lot more profitable things in different walks of life. But there is something absolutely addictive about politics. And it's different to an addiction to power. You can be addicted to politics without having any fucking power at all …

It's the moving and shaking and engaging and intrigue and conspiracies and plotting and one-upmanship and strokes which are an absolute dynamite cocktail …

You're always a lemming heading towards a cliff. There is always an election coming up which might shove you right over the cliff. And that gets you going as well.

*(Senator Joe O'Toole in Katie Hannon's* The Naked Politician*)*

Men are better at fighting for the positions and getting there. Women don't push themselves.

GAA and politics seem to be automatic choices for men.

Any woman who had to balance the budget at home and raise the family gains an automatic organising skill without ever thinking they are learning it.

Men have their shirts ironed for them. They are not too aware of what goes on.

Women have more of the nitty gritty. Men would be better in a broader sense in tackling the issue.

*(Tralee Town Councillor Mary Halloran who, in 1990, was the only woman to hold a political office in Kerry,* The Kerryman, *12 January 1990)*


The thing is to forage between honesty and crookedness and do the best you can.

*(John B. Keane, 'Letters of a Successful TD', in* Celebrated Letters of John B. Keane, *Vol. 1)*


In every country you have had the constitutionalists and the revolutionaries. They are very unhappy partners, but they do produce the end results.

*(Dermot Kinlen in Jimmy Woulfe's* Voices of Kerry*)*

If Ronald Regan can run America at 78, surely I'll manage South Kerry at 72.

*(Veteran Labour Party politician, Michael Moynihan, in the moments after his election to the Dáil in 1989. Quote given to me by John O'Mahony)*


I have worn my front and back teeth talking about it.

*(Cllr Michael Gleeson laments the long-running saga of securing a new public cemetery for Killarney, speaking at a meeting of Killarney District Municipal Authority at Killarney Town Hall on Wednesday 1 April 2015. Recorded by the author)*


I remember cleaning the dump with my late father and the first thing we did in the morning after putting back in the battery was to hit the seat to make sure the rats were gone out from under it.

We didn't get the money or steal it.

*(Cllr Danny Healy-Rae defends the €300k earned by the Healy-Rae firm from Kerry County Council in 2014,* Kerry's Eye, *12 March 2015)*


It's very lucrative, looking at it. By Jesus, the hen is laying well, Councillor Healy-Rae.

*(Cllr Brendan Cronin responds to him,* Kerry's Eye, *12 March 2015)*

The low and contemptible state of your magistracy is the cause of much evil, particularly in the Kingdom of Kerry. I say Kingdom, for it seems absolutely not a part of the same country.

*(John Philpot Curran in the Irish House of Commons on 23 January 1787, parlipapers.chadwyck.com)*

To think that any bird would be foolish enough to build her nest where she'd be blown to pieces and the feathers blown off her and she to be left standing naked in the middle of the road never made sense to me. Birds have brains as well and they will build where it is safe to reproduce and to feel safe.

*(Cllr Danny Healy-Rae responds to criticism of hedge-cutting and burning restrictions under Wildlife Acts at Kerry County Council. Anne Lucey, 'Healy-Rae: Birds have brains as well',* Irish Examiner, *16 December 2014)*

John O'Donoghue told me a long time ago that I wouldn't succeed in politics because I wasn't ruthless enough. You have to be ruthless. When you're in politics, everything else in life becomes secondary. It takes away from the good things in life. It coarsens you. It toughens you. I'm not the Mr Nice Guy that got elected in 1985 … I socialise with people who have no interest in politics. I envy them their naivety.

*(Senator Ned O'Sullivan in Katie Hannon's* The Naked Politician*)*

It is a strange, strange fate, and now, as I stand face to face with death, I feel just as though they were going to kill a boy. For I feel like a boy – and my hands are so free from blood and my heart always so compassionate and pitiful that I cannot comprehend that anyone wants to hang me.

*(Message found in Roger Casement's condemned cell, quoted in Constantia Maxwell's* The Stranger in Ireland. *Casement had been arrested at Banna Strand, Co. Kerry, when he arrived from Germany just before the outbreak of the Easter Rising in 1916)*

If I die, I die in a good cause.

*(Thomas Ashe, the Lord Mayor of Dublin, as he lay dying on 25 September 1917, having been force-fed while on hunger strike with forty other republican prisoners seeking political status in Mountjoy Prison. Seán Ó Luing,* I Die in a Good Cause*)*

The 1930s was the time of the shut mouth and the closed eye and the hardened heart. There were two black clouds covering the pleasant face of the country. One of them was the Catholic Church and the other was the State. They made prisoners of our minds and bodies and 'twas that bleak for a while we were afraid to take note of the beating of our own hearts.

*(John B. Keane,* The Little Book of John B. Keane*)*

An election in most places is an occasion for breaking heads, abusing opponents, and other similar demonstrations of ardent local philanthropy. Such opportunities are never lost by Kerry men, whose heads are harder and whose wits are sharper than those of the average run of humanity. If you are a real Kerry man of respectable convictions, and self-respecting into the bargain, you will never let the man who is drinking with you entertain any opinions but your own at election times. If he contradicts you, it's up with your stick and a crack on his skull and as that only tickles him up – having much the effect of a nettle under a donkey's tail – you then go outside and mutually destroy as much of each other as can be effected in a fight ...

The election was great fun except for the stones and bricks, of which enough were thrown about to build a city without foundations.

*(Samuel Hussey,* The Reminiscences of an Irish Land Agent*)*


I hope that the irony will not be lost upon you, that I stand here on my evening of defeat, in a hall, this magnificent sports complex, which I helped to build.

*(Former Justice Minister and Tánaiste John O'Donoghue, losing his seat in the 2011 general election, addressing the crowd at the €16m Killarney Sports and Leisure Complex, www.politics.ie, 28 February 2011)*

I came into this House an honest man. I never asked anything of any man. I never took anything from any man. I never would. I never could. To do otherwise would be to deny who I am and who I came from. Those who think otherwise do not know me and never will. I will walk proudly out of this Chair, as proud as the day I walked into it …

In the fullness of time, it will become apparent that many matters have been distorted and exaggerated beyond the bounds of fairness. Simple techniques such as aggregating annual expenditures to produce headlines, attributing the costs of other persons' expenditures to the office-holder personally, insinuating that routine decisions in relation to expenses on car-hire or hotels were made or dictated by me, failing to acknowledge that many expenses flowed from well established patterns of official duties such as the St Patrick's Day festival, maliciously suggesting that I attempted to reclaim charitable donations and excessive gratuities, conflation of accommodation charges, and many others were used to create an ugly, grasping, black caricature of the man I am.

*(Caherciveen TD John O'Donoghue resigns as Ceann Comhairle on 13 October 2009, www.oireachtas.ie)*

… yes, indeed, as long as ever I can recollect, I [Daniel O'Connell] always felt a presentiment that I should write my name on the page of history. I hated Saxon domination. I detested the tyrants of Ireland.

In the course of the conversation, I asked him [Daniel O'Connell] who, in his opinion, was our greatest man?

'Next to myself,' he answered, 'I think old Harry Grattan was. But he was decidedly wrong in his controversy with Flood about the simple repeal.'

*(William J. Daunt,* Personal Reflections of the Late Daniel O'Connell, MP*)*


I knew some of those men and had met them socially. It was brought home to me most of all at Jack Lynch's funeral that there was [*sic*] so few really good men in politics. And I always felt that politics was a sort of vocation, particularly socialism. I was in a socialist circle for a great part of my life, even communist, because of the good it would do to your fellow man and that everyone would be brought to the same level, and that there would be no hunger in the world anymore. I was really horrified to find that politicians were really doing these terrible things.

*(Éamon Kelly on revelations of political corruption,* The Kerryman, *19 November 1999)*


Nobody, nobody, nobody will ever bate us.

*(Michael Healy-Rae addressing a packed town square in Kenmare from the back of a lorry following his father's election to Dáil Éireann in 2007,* YouTube, 28 May 2007*)*

Sugar Daddy is back.

> *(Former councillor Niall Botty O'Callaghan introducing Jackie Healy-Rae to the crowd at the same victory rally, YouTube, 28 May 2007)*

I do not take lectures on democracy from a Trotskyite communist like Deputy Joe Higgins.

> *(Justice Minister Michael McDowell, April 2003, www.oireachtas.ie)*

Is the Taoiseach aware that in the United States it is considered that the reason for President Obama's visit is to support his re-election campaign and how this will impact on the Irish American vote? Is it not a little rich that the taxpayer, as well as bailing out European speculators, must now make a contribution to the re-election campaign of a United States President? In view of the fact that the royal family of Britain is one of the wealthiest families in the world and that this country is, figuratively, almost sleeping rough, will the Taoiseach ask the Queen if she might make a contribution towards her own bed and breakfast costs to assist the unfortunate taxpayers and go easier on them?

> *(Deputy Joe Higgins to Taoiseach Enda Kenny in the Dáil in advance of the visits of US President Barack Obama and Queen Elizabeth II to Ireland in 2011. Oireachtas Debates, 20 April 2011, www.oireachtas.ie)*

## THE BODY POLITIC

Kerry was quite equal to current demands on her inhumanity.

A neighbour of the M'Gillycuddys was visited by another Land League detachment and had his ear, *à la* Bulgaria, cut clean off to the bone, because he had worked on a farm from which a tenant had been evicted.

*(Samuel Hussey,* The Reminiscences of an Irish Land Agent*)*


Unless we throw away the measuring stick, neither Oisín nor any one of the Kerry Stars will ever measure up in the eyes of the state.

Oisín hasn't failed. The state has failed him.

What government, what department, or what arm of the state has the right to decide on Oisín's happiness or well-being?

Who wrote the rules that say if you're physically or intellectually challenged in any way, life for you is going to be made harder than it already is? Why do special needs family members still have to beg and bang on doors and shout louder than everybody else just to get basic supports?

Is it because Oisín doesn't need it? Is it because he doesn't deserve it? Or is it because, in the eyes of the state, Oisín doesn't measure up to what the state thinks Oisín should be? ...

All of us can do more. How different life would be were it not for the coaches and volunteers in the Kerry Stars who have literally changed lives. I know the athletes and all family members are eternally grateful ...

Maybe one day, other sporting organisations like the GAA

will follow suit and adopt a real and meaningful approach to sport for all.

On my phone, I still have kept the countless texts from Oisín that ask 'Dad, when can I play for Rathmore', 'When can I play with the minors', 'When can I play for the U-21s'?

I have never answered, because I know what the answer is.

Maybe one day, Liam O'Neill or the Croke Park Executive will come to visit Oisín and give him an answer, an answer as to why the biggest sporting organisation in this country does little or nothing to promote and facilitate GAA for people with special needs.

Oisín has the jersey. He has the socks and the boots. He has the belly for battle. All he's asking for is a chance.

And when all is said and done, that's what it comes down to – a chance. A chance to be the best person you can be and have the best life that can be lived.

That's all it is for the athletes – no different to anybody else.

*(Speech delivered by* Kerry's Eye *journalist Aidan O'Connor in November 2014, at the annual Black Tie dinner of Kerry Stars, of which his son, Oisín, is a member)*


I remember that when de Valera was Taoiseach, he came to the house for lunch on a Sunday and even though it was a Sunday, we got the local creamery opened up so that we could get fresh cream for the Taoiseach. And my abiding memory is of all the women fussing around in the kitchen getting things ready while all the men sat around the table with Dev. Women didn't sit down with the men in those days.

> *(Kay Caball, daughter of the late North Kerry Deputy Dan Moloney, recalls Éamon de Valera's visit to their home in the 1950s, in Owen O'Shea's* Heirs to the Kingdom*)*

While my sisters were interested in swapping fancy paper and playing in the Wendy House, I was more interested in sitting in the kitchen listening to certain discussions that were going on, about maybe something that was happening in South Africa at the time or in the six counties. Or maybe my mother and the next door neighbour crying over how to feed the kids: 'It's Wednesday and my social welfare money is gone.'

> *(Councillor Toiréasa Ferris, daughter of Deputy Martin Ferris, TD, in Owen O'Shea's* Heirs to the Kingdom*)*

Politics was bred into me, it's part of what I am.

> *(Thomas McEllistrim Junior, TD for Kerry North, in Owen O'Shea's* Heirs to the Kingdom*)*

It's in your blood and you would be dying to get back into it. It's like a drug and you can't keep away from it.

> *(Councillor Anne McEllistrim, in Owen O'Shea's* Heirs to the Kingdom*)*

Various world governments will send messages of congratulation to President Bush on his re-election. It should be seen as diplomatic courtesy, without any heartfelt warmth.

The world would be a safer place had President Bush been defeated. Now all we can do is combine with others, using our small piece of rope to help restrain the Gulliver who threatens to trample our little universe.

*(Padraig Kennelly, 'Beating around the Bush. In My Opinion',*
*Kerry's Eye, 4 November 2004)*


I can recall in my earliest years in the Dáil, if there were by-elections, the first they thought of in the party was 'put up the widow'. And I remember an old veteran TD, Martin Corry from East Cork one time when there was a by-election, and he said, 'move the writ and put up the widow'.

*(Former Fianna Fáil TD John O'Leary,*
*in Owen O'Shea's* Heirs to the Kingdom*)*


The people of Britain are not our enemies. They and we have a common foe – the ruthless vested interests that more and more are exploiting us … The first step towards freedom is to realise who are your real enemies.

*(Con Houlihan, 'Freedom is a subtle thing',*
*The Kerryman, February 1974)*

Readers should not get upset at Bertie Ahern on Sunday calling himself a Socialist. He was no different to what he was on Saturday or Monday.

At one time, calling a person a Socialist could be grounds for a slander claim or even worse, internment without trial. When our Taoiseach and former Finance Minister calls himself a Socialist, just remember the years of neglect of the health services, the patients on trolleys and the district hospitals for Tralee and Dingle remaining socialist dreams on paper.

*(Padraig Kennelly, 'In My Opinion',*
Kerry's Eye, *18 November 2004)*


The last thing John B. Keane can ever have expected to happen to him is that he would ever become trendy. He has always survived without the sympathy and admiration of the smart lads up in Dublin and now that they have rediscovered him, he has been careful to keep his distance, refusing even to attend rehearsals of his plays at the Abbey …

Keane has been a social critic, and he has contributed to a greater freedom of expression about sexual matters in rural Ireland. But he has done his critique of rural society in the name of what are basically good old-fashioned conservative values. He is at heart a typical Fine Gael small businessman from a small Irish town.

*(*The Phoenix, *19 June 1987)*

It was sometimes political, sometimes social, but no matter what it was, it was always brilliant. In those days, that single column seemed to have been his [Con Houlihan's] week's work. He started it over a bottle of Guinness and a Black Bush in the Brogue Inn and he might take two or three days to finish it.

He weighed every word he wrote and every word was weighty. He was fearless. We mightn't always have agreed with what he wrote but we certainly defended his right to write it.

*(Seamus McConville,* The Kerryman, *19 June 1998)*

'Publish Con Houlihan's article this week and you can make your last confession.' The anonymous call came at ten-twenty on the first Monday morning of February 1974, less than an hour after I had taken over the editorial chair at *The Kerryman* …

A chat with Tony Meade, the paper's deputy editor and editorial page editor, confirmed that Con was writing about the campaign to have the Price sisters, Dolores and Marian, returned to the north to serve out sentences imposed on them in a British court …

Every van leaving *The Kerryman* building in Clash the next day had a garda escort. All papers were delivered without incident.

*(Seamus McConville, 'The freedom to speak',*
The Kerryman 1904–2004 *anniversary publication)*

After a few years of my involvement with *The Kerryman*, the good Con Casey retired … His successor, Seamus McConville, was equally liberal and possibly even braver: the alleged IRA – both factions – were now at their most virulent.

We survived. All I can say in my defence is that I could see then what it took many people about a quarter of a century to see.

I put it very simply: every bullet and every bomb militated against the concept of a united Ireland, even if that dream could ever become flesh.

*(Con Houlihan, 'The Kerryman who wouldn't be gagged',
in* Windfalls*)*


To give leprechauns the right to vote. To build a factory for shaving the hair off gooseberries. To give free treatment for sick heads after the night before. To salvage the skins of black puddings after the contents had been eaten.

*(Election manifesto delivered in Listowel in May 1951 by 'Thomas Xavier Doodle', an election candidate invented by John B. Keane to take the bitterness out of Irish politics.* A Tribute to John B. Keane, *supplement to* The Kerryman, *12 February 1999)*

I think people have taken out on Charlie what they might have looked at in themselves. He is an ard rí. I think he sees himself like an emperor. He likes land and big houses and money. He does. But I'm talking about something essential in him. He can recite Latin poetry. I think he is a kind man.

*(Brendan Kennelly's estimation of Charlie Haughey, quoted by Justine McCarthy in an article, 'The Keeper of the Flame',* Irish Independent, *4 July 2001)*

Many backbenchers were in fear of him [Haughey] because, if you spoke out against him, he could make sure you would be isolated and sidelined. But the bitterness and division wasn't just in the parliamentary party. Some of Haughey's supporters were an intimidating lot; they would appear in the Dáil bar late at night and many of them can only be described as thugs. Especially if there was a heave against him, a lot of party members who were pro-Haughey would be seen around Leinster House, pressuring TDs into supporting their man. They would turn up from the Dublin constituencies, as well as pro-Haughey members of the National Executive and they would crowd around the bar or the entrance to Leinster House to intimidate backbenchers. They were like a mafia.

*(John O'Leary,* On the Doorsteps: Memoirs of a Long-serving TD*)*

This government has put our country into a political, economic and social state of deep crisis. We are impoverished at home and humiliated abroad.

What is needed is for the Labour Party to see clearly what they are doing to the economy by continuing to support this government.

To see the hardship they are inflicting on Social Welfare recipients, to see the cutbacks that are being made in the semi-state sector, and to decide this is not a right or natural role for a Labour Party to be playing.

Reasonable economy can be accepted by the community but what we are witnessing now is a complete dismantling of the Health Service. It's the job of the State to provide a reasonable standard of health services.

*('Haughey slams Coalition in Killarney speech',*
*The Kerryman, 21 December 1984)*

'Will I get in this time?' the sitting MP said once to one of our neighbours, coming up to polling day.

'Of course you will,' the neighbour told him. 'Didn't you say yourself that it was the poor put you in the last time and aren't there twice as many poor there now.'

*(Éamon Kelly,* The Apprentice*)*

Dick Spring, Rock Street Branch.

> *(The Labour leader's introduction to what was arguably his best speech ever, delivered at the 1987 party conference in Cork. Stephen Collins,* Spring and the Labour Story*)*

The leadership came about ten years earlier than I planned it … I had planned to be leader. I had actually put a bet on in my Trinity days that I was going to lead the party and I collected it too. A long time later but I got my £50 from quite a successful businessman. That was an ambitious bet back around 1972 …

I had the curious situation of trying to appeal to the voters of Castleisland and all they wanted was a mains drainage scheme while the BBC were trying to follow me to find out what I was about. And you were conscious of wanting to avoid sending out to the world the signal that the issue in the election was a drainage scheme or whatever.

> *(Dick Spring in Stephen Collins'* Spring and the Labour Story*)*

This debate is not about Brian Lenihan when it is all boiled down. This debate, essentially, is about the evil spirit that controls one political party in this Republic, and it is about the way in which that spirit has begun to corrupt the entire political system in our country. This is a debate about greed for office, about disregard for truth and about contempt for political standards. It is a debate about the way in which a once-great party has been brought to its knees by the grasping acquisitiveness of its leader. It is ultimately a debate about the cancer that is eating away at our body politic and the virus which has caused that cancer. An Taoiseach, Charles J. Haughey.

*(Dick Spring, Dáil debate on the presidential campaign, Oireachtas Debates, www.oireachtas.ie, 31 October 1990)*


Dick Spring at the age of thirty-two, with just eighteen months' experience as a TD and just one month as party leader, was now Tánaiste. It had been an extraordinary rise in the political world and would have been an extraordinary rise for anybody, let alone someone of his limited political experience. He joked that he had gone from being a barman in New York to being Tánaiste all in the space of a couple of years ...

*(Stephen Collins,* Spring and the Labour Story*)*


A sheep in sheep's clothing.

*(Peter Barry on Dick Spring in Stephen Collins'* Spring and the Labour Story*)*


You go forth from this court with no stain on your character except that of having been acquitted by a Kerry jury.

*(Source unknown)*

Kerry is great fun in court. The late State Solicitor, Donie Browne, used to say it was practically impossible to get a conviction in Kerry. I used to think this was due to my brilliance as a defence counsel. But I later discovered it was as much due to the desire of Kerry juries to release people.

*(Dermot Kinlen in Jimmy Woulfe's* Voices of Kerry*)*


Let them go to the Circuit Court where right of way is dealt with and not be wasting this court's time and annoying the guards who have enough to do.

*(District Judge Humphrey Kelleher, 'Go to the circuit court – Justice',*
*The Kerryman, 18 September 1987)*


Put up your best witness.

*(A favourite saying of Judge Humphrey Kelleher's at the District Court sessions during the 1980s and 1990s. It was often quoted by solicitors and journalists because it conveyed a characteristic impatience with verbosity and his preference for cutting to the chase)*


There are ways of dealing with matters of people getting a crack of a stone at the back of the head but there's more than one way of skinning a cat! Strike out for want of jurisdiction.

*(District Judge Humphrey Kelleher, 'Assault case in wrong court',*
*The Kerryman, 18 September 1987)*

It was generally accepted that time that only people with political affiliations should almost be entitled to run for the County Council and I said, 'That's ridiculous.'

If I had known how strongly tied the vast majority of households were at the time, I wouldn't have chanced it because it opened my eyes …

Clinics and clientelism and bending the rules is not for me.

*(Football legend Mick O'Connell, who was an independent member of Kerry County Council from 1979 to 1985,* The Kerryman, *18 February 2000)*

These happenings were not a result of recent knowledge coming to the attention of the bishops. It was instead a result of near revolt against the clergy by victims of abuse, persons in responsible positions and the media.

The pressure on the hierarchy was no less than the pressure that collapsed the Iron Curtain that kept the people of Eastern Europe prisoners since the start of the Cold War and the effects were also similar.

The silence from the State and the Justice Department on their mishandling of criminal complaints must now be subjected to similar pressure.

*(Comment by child abuse survivor John Prior, Tralee, in the wake of an order by the Catholic Church to carry out an audit of child abuse in each county. 'A week is a long time for those who should have acted against child abusers',* Kerry's Eye, *11 April 2002)*

A couple of months later, in April 1967, there was great excitement in the town because an American actress, Jayne Mansfield, was coming to Tralee to perform a show …

Increasing pressure was brought to bear on the management of the Mount Brandon Hotel to cancel her show. I couldn't help thinking that only up the road from the hotel was St Joseph's Industrial School, where moral degradation of young innocent boys was being carried out daily by men of the cloth.

*(Michael Clemenger,* Holy Terrors. A Boy. Two Brothers. A Stolen Childhood*)*


Before I visit the Giant's Causeway, I wished to see Ireland's Giant.

*(H. L. H. Von Pueckler-Muskau when asked by Daniel O'Connell if he had been to the Causeway. 'Irish Quotations', in Constantia Maxwell's* The Stranger in Ireland*)*


*A selection of quotes from Sir Richard Boyle Roche (1743–1807), Member of Parliament for Tralee in the House of Commons (1790–1797)*:

The cup of Ireland's misery has been overflowing for a century and is not yet half full.

Why should we do anything for posterity? What has posterity ever done for us?

Half the lies our opponents tell about us are untrue.

The only thing to prevent what's past is to put a stop to it before it happens.

While I write this letter, I have a pistol in one hand and a sword in the other.

I answer boldly in the affirmative: No.

*(Quotes selected from* 'Irish Bull' *by Hal Gordon,* punditwire.com, *16 March 2011)*

# A KERRY CHARACTER: JACKIE HEALY-RAE

Kerry may be a county that is rich in beauty. But beauty never boiled the pot.

*(Jackie Healy-Rae,* The Kerryman, *1 January 1999)*

A date with Jackie Healy-Rae is an appointment with chaos ... Healy-Rae is the kingdom's kingmaker, the Cardinal Richelieu of the MacGillycuddy Reeks.

*(Liam Fay, 'The Kingdom's Kingmaker',* Hot Press, *31 May 1995)*

I wouldn't cut, shovel or dig with him.

*(J. H.-R.'s declaration after Albert Reynolds was appointed Fianna Fáil leader, as quoted by Liam Fay in 'The Kingdom's Kingmaker',* Hot Press, *31 May 1995)*

They'll dance to my music before this is all over.

*(J. H.-R.'s warning to Bertie Ahern and John O'Donoghue after he was excluded from running for election in 1997. Donal Hickey,* The Mighty Healy-Rae*)*

I had a deep and very good respect for him [Bertie Ahern] when he was Minister for Finance. But my view is that, looking down the road that's in front of us, he'll have to tighten up those reins and firm up the structure and maybe torpedo a few chiefs that he has on his front bench.

*(J. H.-R.'s forecast for Bertie Ahern's leadership, as quoted by Liam Fay in 'The Kingdom's Kingmaker',* Hot Press, *31 May 1995)*

The extraordinary thing about it, Liam, is that I never regretted that. I'm a terribly busy person. For that reason, I don't feel one bit worried to see these fellas shaping out for the train on a Tuesday morning and coming back on a Thursday night. Of course, if the opportunity had come my way I'd certainly have gone, no doubt in the world about it, but I was quite happy, and too busy to be otherwise.

*(J. H.-R.'s response to Liam Fay, when asked if he wished he had made it to the Dáil and perhaps even risen to ministerial rank,* Hot Press, *31 May 1995)*

It was spectacular. A tour of the Ring of Kerry with cars and lorries and vans and motorcycles. With loudspeakers and sirens. We gave Cahirciveen [the home ground of his arch rival, Fianna Fáil minister John O'Donoghue] a desperate roasting altogether.

*(J. H.-R. in Katie Hannon's* The Naked Politician*)*

In Rae's early years as a councillor he had a penchant for grabbing headlines by saying something outlandish. Moving a motion calling for the eradication of rats from a dump near Killarney, he said that rats were saluting him on the road every morning he went to a council meeting and even more of them were out as he returned in the evening. Then the county engineer Peter Malone replied that he travelled the same road every day and never saw a single rat. A headline in that week's *Kerryman* read: 'Rats recognise councillor but not county engineer'.

*(Donal Hickey,* The Mighty Healy-Rae*)*

The national hero of the June 1997 Dáil election was wonder boy Independent Jackie Healy-Rae who, at an uncertain age between 59 and 72, managed to outshine all other South Kerry candidates ... He focused on the twenty-year-old voters and won them to his heart.

*(Padraig Kennelly,* Kerry's Eye, *12 June 1997)*

It was like Puck Fair, the Rose of Tralee Festival and a Kerry welcome for the Sam Maguire Cup all rolled into one. The party went on for weeks as Healy-Rae went back over the potholed roads to the villages and parishes that had sent him to Leinster House with such a resounding mandate.

*(Donal Hickey,* The Mighty Healy-Rae*)*

I don't know ye from the man in the moon but I know ye'd have voted for me if ye could. (To a bus of tourists at Loo Bridge.)

*(J. H.-R. in Donal Hickey's* The Mighty Healy-Rae*)*


I have about a half dozen Russian hats. When I'm going to funerals, I'll always wear one of my Russian hats. If I'm fooling around at home, I'll wear any cap or hat at all. I'm wearing the Russian hats a long, long time now. They became a sort of trademark.

*(J. H.-R. in Liam Fay's 'The Kingdom's Kingmaker',*
Hot Press, *31 May 1995)*


One day four years ago his long-time friend Kathleen Cahill, who got tired of looking at the Russian hat, decided a change of style was needed. So off she went into Killarney and picked out the tartan. 'I thought it very smart and just the thing to match Jackie's lively personality. It just caught my eye,' she says.

*(Donal Hickey,* The Mighty Healy-Rae*)*


The Healy-Rae thatch is truly one of the Seven Wonders of the Modern World. Like all great marvels, it comes in many guises. Every angle from which it is examined offers a different view. Jackie's scalp has more beautifully appointed strands than the entire Kerry coastal region ... Anyone who saw Healy-Rae's recent appearance on *The Late Late Show*, however, will be aware that his tresses have at least one further incarnation. On that night, Jackie held a disbelieving nation spellbound with a matted mop that resembled an oil spill and threatened to engulf his entire face before our very eyes.

*(Liam Fay, 'The Kingdom's Kingmaker', Hot Press, 31 May 1995)*

The fellas inside there [Dáil Éireann] can be getting oil for the chains of their bikes.

*(J. H.-R. threatens to withdraw his support for the government and force an election. Donal Hickey,* The Mighty Healy-Rae*)*

I was highly blackguarded the last time by Fianna Fáil. They put out a rumour that's impossible to fight. You can do it once but you can't do it to the same person again. That he's dead safe. There's no reason for voting for him because he's there anyway.

Fianna Fáil have really let me down very badly. The last election was the most hurtful. After the performance I put up for five years and I saved their neck hundreds of times. And Jesus they really made an almighty attempt to get rid of me. I'd have it in my nose for them, of course I would. Don't have any doubt about it. I'd never again be the very same as I was with them. I mean, Jesus, they tried to hurt me to the very roots.

*(J. H.-R. in Katie Hannon's* The Naked Politician*)*

Up the country, there have been over-passes, under-passes and all sorts of passes built with European money. Some of this money should have come to Kerry. Now, we might get our share.

*(The Kerryman, 27 November 1998. J. H.-R. won electoral support by fighting for increased government spend on infrastructure in south Kerry. He made political capital out of potholes in particular!)*

### Jackie Healy-Rae Thy Kingdom 1

*(Banner at Killarney railway station when the politician returned home, having achieved Objective One status for Kerry,*
The Kerryman, *27 November 1998)*

If he [Ahern] wants my support he'll have to come down here and listen to what I want and only then will I make up my mind. I won't be running up to Dublin with finger up saying, 'Bertie, I'm with you all the way.'

I'm not going to vote for the government unless my demands are met. I'm not wavering an inch and am standing firm as the Rock of Cashel.

If that's the way he wants it he can whistle his ducks to water.

*(Response to RTÉ reporter Geraldine Harney's question as to his reaction if Bertie Ahern would not be prepared to do a deal in return for his support for his bid to become Taoiseach.*
Donal Hickey, The Mighty Healy-Rae*)*

Don't write me off. I'm warning ye.

> *(J. H.-R. concluding his maiden speech to the Dáil on Thursday 26 June 1997, Oireachtas Debates, www.oireachtas.ie)*

Some people coming to me are so poor that they couldn't buy a jacket for a gooseberry.

> *(Donal Hickey,* The Mighty Healy-Rae*)*

I told them not to underestimate him and that they were listening to a man from the real Ireland who spoke like a man from the real Ireland. I'd have said the same thing if it was a Fine Gael or Labour TD from South Kerry they were laughing at. When they laughed at Healy-Rae I felt they were also laughing at me and all belonging to me.

> *(Reaction in Leinster House of Kerryman Bart Cronin, former press adviser to several ministers and a worker in the Fianna Fáil campaign. Donal Hickey,* The Mighty Healy-Rae*)*

Almighty Christ, they're after electing a banjo in Clare.

> *(J. H.-R.'s reaction when South African-born psychiatrist Moosajee Bhamjee was elected as TD in 1992. Donal Hickey,* The Mighty Healy-Rae*)*

I had some fierce escapes from dogs but I nearly bled to death after the cock drove his beak through my shoe and cut the vein. I bate the bejabers out of him.

*(J. H.-R. on an attack by a farmyard cock in the Black Valley. Donal Hickey,* The Mighty Healy-Rae*)*


I never saw him [Haughey] putting a pound foolish or buying drinks for people. I was often in his company and I don't think he ever stood me a drink – not that I wanted it from the man. Not alone did he leave me down because of the way he performed, he also let many of his own friends and associates down. The kind of people I represent include small shopkeepers who are finding it very hard to stay in business because of very strict tax regulations. Their turnover is so small they can hardly pay their taxes. To think that a man of his standing couldn't pay taxes makes me feel very sore about it. On the other hand there's no way in the world I can understand how anyone in the world, even Ben Dunne, could call into Haughey on his way home from a golf outing, take three huge bank drafts out of his back pocket and hand them to him because Haughey looked very down and out. How can any man in my shoes understand that? It doesn't add up at all.

*(Donal Hickey,* The Mighty Healy-Rae*)*

Sure am I not propping him up and keeping him in his state car? I don't want to see him walking out of Killarney to Cahirciveen without his car. He should have no problem with me. Sure I'm the most valuable man he has. Am I not one of the three wheels under the government?

*(On former Justice Minister John O'Donoghue, in Donal Hickey's* The Mighty Healy-Rae)

I congratulate the Ceann Comhairle in a very special way. I congratulate him because I go back to when I directed elections for him in the early years. God knows, I played a leading role in sending him to this House in the first instance. I wish him many long and happy years in the seat in which he is now sitting. Standing here this evening, I guarantee the Ceann Comhairle that if there is a bad pothole around Waterville, on Dursey Island in west County Cork or anywhere in Cahirciveen, I will do my very best … in the Ceann Comhairle's absence, I will do my best to sort them out and I will keep him well-informed all the time.

*(J. H.-R. addressing Deputy John O'Donoghue in Leinster House on 14 June 2007 on his appointment as Ceann Comhairle, Oireachtas Debates, www.oireachtas.ie)*

I assure the Deputy that I will never be far away.

*(John O'Donoghue's response)*

I see no reason in the world why we shouldn't try nudist beaches. If people want to go without clothes why should they be made wear them? It's up to themselves in a secured beach in Ballybunion. We're not living in the grey old ages for God Almighty's sake. There's a massive market for this and that's why I have no objection to it. It's a modern world and we'll have to keep up with the rest of them. Let Peeping Toms and Holy Joes keep out, there is no obligation on them to go there anyway.

*(Donal Hickey,* The Mighty Healy-Rae*)*

# A SENSE OF PLACE

I had a feeling then that there was magic and mystery everywhere, that I lived in a magic place. I felt it even though I did not know then that I lived in the oldest land. I did not know then that ten thousand years ago, when the great ice cap melted and moved south, it left my North Kerry homeland untouched. Was this why the ghosts of time were always moving in my head, the ghosts of ancient time, the time before the melting ice came down?

*(Rory O'Connor,* Gander at the Gate*)*


And there is that place called Kerry. You have to come from outside to fully appreciate its magic ...

If I were to choose a place which has special memories for me it would be Caherdaniel. That's where we spent our summers when our children were small: caravanning at Dan Curran's in Glenbeg ...

Good friends have made it easy to live here, to take root. We thank God every day for their generosity! It is what binds us to the sainted soil of Kerry.

*(Seamus McConville in Valerie O'Sullivan's* I am of Kerry*)*

Inch. What a funny little name for such a stupendous place. I remembered how, on our first time-stopped day, the car climbed the hill and we drove through the tunnel of hedges into a secret garden. Just to hear the word 'Inch' and I was, for a moment, back inside my magic bubble.

*(Annie Murphy,* Forbidden Fruit*)*


Ballinskelligs is part of the topography of Heaven.

*(Terri Leddy, 'Letters and Verses', in Finbarr Bracken's* Ballinskelligs Remembered*)*


As I write I'm looking out over Ballinskelligs Bay. It was here, we are told, that Clanna Mhíleadh, the first Celtic invaders set foot in Ireland. And here, Amergin, a son of Milesius, recited his famous incantatory poem in which he identifies with the landscape, animal life and the very life force itself:

*Mé gaeth ar muir*
*Mé seig i n-aill ...*

*(Paddy Bushe, 'The Poet as Blow-In', in Gabriel Fitzmaurice's* Kerry Through Its Writers*)*


Do I not meet scores of people who tell me they would love to go to Kerry, but they have never been nearer than Killarney?

*(Samuel Hussey,* The Reminiscences of an Irish Land Agent*)*

His prospects were all before him like a beggarman looking down on Killarney.

*(Anon)*

Killarney is the graveyard of ambition.

*(Anon)*

The French monarch might possibly be able to erect another Versailles, but could not with all his revenues lay out another Muckross.

*(An eighteenth-century visitor to Killarney quoted by Charles Smith in* The Ancient and Present State of the County of Kerry*)*

A place so lovely that it seems,
Neither from waking life nor dreams,
A mystery from those mysteries,
That startle shut and waking eyes.

*(Lines written by W. B. Yeats in the Muckross House visitors' book in August 1926, and now inscribed on the floor of a gazebo in the gardens)*

Next to you and my babes, I love Iveragh.

*(Daniel O'Connell in a letter to his wife, Mary, in March 1810, quoted in Crowley and Sheehan,* The Iveragh Peninsula: A Cultural Atlas of the Ring of Kerry*)*

I give a big cheer when I am down in Iveragh each time I go into the sea for a swim at Coos Crom or off Valentia Island. I holiday there and we have a premises there. I go down as often as I can get out of Dublin. There is always some new mountain to be climbed or some fresh discovery. My idyllic day in Kerry would be a day out on the sea with my pals, Mick O'Connell and Ned Fitzgerald, heading for the Skelligs or the Blaskets. That would rank high. Another would be to climb Carrauntoohil or Mount Brandon or our holy mountain of Caherciveen, Cnoc na dTobar. The third idyllic day would be to attend the Munster Final in Killarney with Kerry having a comfortable lead with ten minutes to go so that there would be time to take in the scenery; another would be a day at Ballybunion Golf Course and to have the privilege of having a birdie at any hole there!

*(Hugh O'Flaherty in Jimmy Woulfe's* Voices of Kerry*)*


More than 200 metres high, thirteen kilometres offshore, Skellig Michael is the true end – or the beginning? – of the Iveragh range, a half-drowned mountain serving time as an island until geology crumples and the seabed heaves again.

In the meantime, there is so much high ground heaped up on the peninsula that it spills out over the Atlantic coast and gets its feet wet.

*(Dermot Somers, 'The Mountains of Iveragh: A Personal Journey', in Crowley and Sheehan,* The Iveragh Peninsula: A Cultural Atlas of the Ring of Kerry*)*

'Those Skelligs,' said an imaginative English visitor, 'are like two huge cathedrals rising out of the sea.'

*(William J. Daunt,* Personal Recollections of the Late Daniel O'Connell, MP*)*


Round the corner, in the front bar of the Killarney Grand, a saintly-looking young woman and a rather debauched-looking young man are playing fiddle and guitar. Immediately in front of them, several rows of French, Italian and Scandinavian tourists sit and stare in reverential silence. One of them is taping the session. Behind them stand the English, Americans and Australians, listening all right, but also occasionally chatting, much to the annoyance of a sour-faced, curly-haired Viking in cycling shorts, who keeps shushing Nordically. Further back still, stretching the full length of the enormous and luxuriously refitted bar, stand the young professional Irish, chattering like speed freaks and ignoring the music completely, as they discuss work and house prices while trying to get off with each other.

*(Pete McCarthy,* McCarthy's Bar*)*


'Say farewell to Ireland,' cries one of the rowers, and I turn and bid farewell, not only to Ireland, but to England and Europe and all the tangled world of today.

*(Robin Flower referring to a boat journey to the Great Blasket, in* The Western Island*)*

## A Sense of Place

We thought we were special, we who lived on the Blaskets, and indeed there were fine men and women on the island. There was no doctor, no nurse, no shop, no Post Office, no horses, even. And yet we never felt deprived.

*(Máirín Ní Dhuinnshléibhe, Bean Uí Bheoláin, in Brenda Ní Shúilleabháin's* Bibeanna: Memories from a Corner of Ireland*)*


Scríobhas go mionchruinn ar a lán gcúrsaí d'fhonn go mbeadh cuimhne i bpoll éigin orthu agus thugas iarracht ar mheon na ndaoine a bhí i mo thimpeall a chur síos chun go mbeadh a dtuairisc inár ndiaidh, mar ná beidh ár leithéidí arís ann.

I have written minutely of much that we did, for it was my wish that somewhere there should be a memorial of it all, and I have done my best to set down the character of the people about me so that some record of us might live after us, for the like of us will never be again.

*(Tomás Ó Criomhthain,* An tOileánach,
*praising the people of the Blaskets)*


Crag Cave is a prelude to eternity's wonders.

*(Éamon Keane in a comment in the visitors' book at the cave)*

A great place for smuggling, altogether, and the whole of Dingle built upon it, you might say. They were all in it here, from the highest to the lowest, and the magistrates often enough winked at it themselves.

*(Related by 'John', a guide, to Richard Hayward, quoted in* In the Kingdom of Kerry*)*


Port used to come direct to Dingle. It was an easy harbour 'to run', and there was some smuggling.

On one occasion some soldiers were sent to protect the gauger, who was bent on making an important seizure. A few of the inhabitants of Dingle took the opportunity of entertaining the officer, and whilst he slumbered from the effects of their hospitality, the opportunity for making the seizure was lost.

*(Samuel Hussey,* The Reminiscences of an Irish Land Agent*)*


Castle Island has been described as a street amidst the fields. It is still true. Most of the houses have fields coming up to their back. And nobody is surprised to find a hare eating his cabbage at dawn. The rabbits come too, but rabbits prefer lettuce. There was a time when wolves roamed the streets, but by the end of the nineteenth century the wolves had been wiped out.

*(Con Houlihan, 'Wolves',* Herald.ie/columnist, *26 October 2011)*

To most people, The Fountain is the town's focus, but my focus is hardly in the town at all; it is the spot where Creamery Lane, now gone upmarket as Convent View, meets our beloved Maine. There, at the Nuns' Pool, I have often gone to refresh my spirit.

It is probably my favourite spot in the whole world. The Australian Aborigines would understand. They have their sacred places: Ayers Rock is to them as the Nuns' Pool is to me.

*(Con Houlihan writing about Castleisland, in Con Houlihan's Ireland – The Lost Essays,* Irish Independent, *2 March 2013)*


Mary is from Knocknagoshel. Some people say that Knocknagoshel is a state onto [*sic*] itself. That it belongs to no particular continent, world or planet. So she is a very independent-minded woman like all Knocknagoshel people. But in common with all Knocknagoshel people, she has great charm and is a great worker and she gave me the opportunity to write.

*(John B. Keane writing about his wife, in Jimmy Woulfe's* Voices of Kerry*)*


Listowel is a town with a lot of clever, sharp, smart, quick-tongued townies.

*(Brendan Kennelly,* The Kerryman, *12 February 1999)*

Listowel, the town I had chosen to settle in, could be compared to a greying doxy guarding the roads from Limerick to Tralee. When I first saw her she was perfumed with beer and beefburger and bedecked with bunting as she played host to one of the many all-Ireland Fleadhanna held there.

As a refugee from the spiritual Chernobyl of Fermanagh, I found her warmhearted and gracious. She was welcoming and enticing. I vowed on our first meeting that I would eventually return.

*(Mickey McConnell, 'Kerry', in Gabriel Fitzmaurice's* Kerry Through Its Writers*)*

Puck Fair is the great annual fete and mart of Killorglin; and it is so called because a goat is always fastened to a stave on a platform, and gaily bedizened. Formerly the animal was attached to the flagstaff on the Castle. To this fair all Kerry for many miles congregates, and the neighbouring roads towards evening are liberally strewn with bibulous individuals of either sex.

*(Samuel Hussey,* The Reminiscences of an Irish Land Agent*)*

My body to Ireland, my heart to Rome, and my soul to God.

*(Daniel O'Connell's last words in Genoa on 15 May 1847)*

The flatlands of the Maharees on the Dingle peninsula boasts Fermoyle strand which is overshadowed by Mount Brandon called after Saint Brendan the Navigator, patron saint of Kerry and discoverer of America whatever the Spanish might say. These golden sands enchant the holidaymaker who seeks peace and solitude.

*(John B. Keane, 'The Kingdom of God and the Kingdom of Kerry', in Gabriel Fitzmaurice's* Kerry Through Its Writers*)*

When my father said we were moving to Ballybunion, it was almost impossible to take in. I can only remember desperate, piercing happiness. For us Ballybunion was the most rapturous place. The sun always shone. We always had picnics. There was ice-cream. There were swings, roundabouts, travelling players who stayed for the summer. It surged with energy and bustle. The big hotels were the most exotic and untouchable things on earth. The sea was there, always. We ran out and told everybody and everybody was static with jealousy.

*(Mary Cummins, 'The Sergeant', in Gabriel Fitzmaurice's* Kerry Through Its Writers*)*

Born by the sea, one never loses the sound of the sea and the majestic Shannon estuary at Tarbert was a continual fascination in a whole variety of ways. There was swimming in the favoured spots such as Rusheen, Wall's Bay, the Slatey Pier, the Island and the Back-o-the-hill. There was fishing from the pier and on 'The Bank'. Periwinkles, bornachs and mussels were in profusion and unpolluted among the shores. The tides came and went in ceaseless motion, ships plied up and down the river, and the curlews, seagulls, swans and widgeon brought the reed-fringed mudflats and creeks to life.

*(John Coolahan, 'Growing up in a North Kerry Village', in Gabriel Fitzmaurice's* Kerry Through Its Writers*)*

A few years ago there was hardly a plough, car or carriage of any kind; the butter, the only produce, was carried to Cork on horseback; there was not a decent public-house, and I think only one house slated and plastered in the village of Cahersiveen.

*(Engineer Alexander Nimmo in a report to his superiors on 1 March 1824)*

'Níor dheaghaigh éinne go Bólas gan dóchas rud d'fháil ann' is an old local proverb that can still be heard in Iveragh today. It could be translated as 'nobody ever went to Bólas without hope of finding something in there'.

*(Seán Mac an tSíthigh, 'Uíbh Ráthach and the Evolution of Irish Folklore', in Crowley and Sheehan,* The Iveragh Peninsula: A Cultural Atlas of the Ring of Kerry*)*

# A Sense of Place

Waterville is a straggling eyeful of beauty most romantically placed at the north-east corner of Ballinskelligs Bay, an almost circular piece of the Atlantic which takes its name from the Skelligs …

*(Richard Hayward,* In the Kingdom of Kerry*)*


The Stacks Mountains is to John B. what Dublin is to James Joyce: a real physical place, but also a mythical place in his head, populated by fascinating women and men who demand full dramatic expression.

*(Brendan Kennelly,* The Kerryman, *12 February 1999)*


Locally, I recall a trip around Kilgarvan with Denis P. O'Sullivan when I met with poitín makers, storytellers and singers and learned a lot of the history of that lovely place. This was a sort of a portrait-of-a-locality venture. Denis would talk of the old butter road to Cork as though it had been used in his own time. Then there were Pauline and Paddy Maguire in the Anchor Bar in Cahirciveen, always welcoming and with a finger on the pulse of local happenings.

*(Tony Meade,* The Kerryman 1904–2004 *anniversary publication)*


Valentia is alive with the business connected with the fishing industry and very good wages are paid to all employed in boxing and removing the fish to the railway station for conveyance to the English markets. Some is also sent by steamer to England. Two Norwegian barges have come with cargoes of ice. Valentia has established itself as a great fishing station.

*(The Kerry Sentinel, 25 April 1900)*


I must take an early train to Kerry because the instinct of a wounded animal is to return to its nest.

*(John Moriarty referring to his cancer treatment in Dublin, in Micheál Ó Muircheartaigh's* From Borroloola to Mangerton Mountain*)*

# SPORTING DAYS

Pride lads, what is pride? I'll tell you now. Pride is when your mother puts your football boots out on the window ledge on a Monday and the dirt is still on them. And when people go past the house they don't see the unwashed boots. They see boots with the Croke Park sod on them. That's what pride is …

In Kerry we start out every year with the same ambition; to win the All-Ireland. That is what the people expect. And that is all I have to say on the matter.

*(Páidí Ó Sé in Donal Keenan's* Páidí: A Big Life*)*

Football is different here. People say that about a lot of places, but in Kerry it is true. Football matters here more than it does anywhere else. It's bred into the bone, taught from the cradle. When we train in Killarney we do so with the stark grey buildings of St Finian's [*sic*] mental hospital looming over us. Johnny Culloty, my friend and selector, whose working life was spent in there, often points out that in a good year, when Kerry win the All-Ireland, admissions would go down. A bad year is one where we don't win the All-Ireland.

*(Jack O'Connor,* The Keys to the Kingdom*)*

A Kerry footballer with an inferiority complex is one who thinks he's just as good as everybody else.

*(John B. Keane, a quote given to me by his son Billy)*


Only for I have respect for the wall there, I'd spatter your blood up against it.

*(One delegate shouting to another from the same parish at a 1960s County Board Meeting recalled by sports editor John Barry in 'Just the ticket', The Kerryman 1904–2004 anniversary publication)*


You would learn more at one Kerry selection committee meeting than at all the universities going.

*(Mickey Ned O'Sullivan, who succeeded Mick O'Dwyer as Kerry football trainer/manager, The Kerryman, 5 January 1990)*


When playing with Kerry, especially at senior championship level, I always felt an extra sense of responsibility and desire to win: it was as if there was more at stake than the game of football itself, and the team was carrying the hopes and aspirations of thousands of Kerry men and women, at home and abroad.

*(Jimmy Deenihan,* My Sporting Life*)*

Johneen a chroí, don't take that job at all, they'll all be giving out to you.

*(Jack O'Connor's mother's words to him, having just heard that he was to be appointed Kerry senior manager,* The Keys to the Kingdom*)*


Kerry people think, or should I say know, that they have a divine right to win All-Irelands and it's not so great for a lad like me coming in at the bottom ...

I am not naïve enough to think that we can put eleven new lads into a team and win the All-Ireland.

*(Mickey Ned O'Sullivan,* The Kerryman, *5 January 1990)*


A high lobbing, dropping ball in towards the goalmouth ... a shot ... a goal, a goal, a goal for Offaly. There was a goal in it.

*(GAA broadcaster Micheál Ó Hehir on that infamous Seamus Derby goal for Offaly in 1982 which deprived Kerry of the elusive five-in-a-row, www.independent.ie/sport)*


Many players mistake vigour for skill, and retaliation for proof of superiority. And a team that excels itself in manly straight-forward play may lose and still surpass their opponents.

*(Dr Eamonn O'Sullivan in Weeshie Fogarty's* Dr Eamonn O'Sullivan: A Man Before His Time*)*

Mike Sheehy was running up to take the kick – and suddenly Paddy [Cullen] dashed back towards his goal like a woman who smells a cake burning. The ball won the race and it curled inside the near post as Paddy crashed into the outside of the net and lay against it like a fireman who had returned to find his station ablaze.

*(Con Houlihan's report on the Kerry/Dublin All-Ireland,* The Evening Press, *1978)*

Whenever I met him, I told him that he was the best player I ever saw, simply because the harder they hit him, the better he played.

*(Veteran Kerry star Martin 'Bracker' Regan explains why he thought Strand Road player John Dowling was the greatest,* Kerry's Eye, *23 September 2004)*

It's a totally different game today than when I played. The ball was heavy leather with a red bladder and laced up and when it was kicked over your head it would make a whistling sound.

I remember one day, playing back in Dingle, Paddy Bawn Brosnan put out his hand to stop a ball going past him and it broke his fingers.

*(Martin 'Bracker' Regan,* Kerry's Eye, *23 September 2004)*

A handy farmer would make a tidy living in the amount of ground it took you to turn in.

*(Kerry player Johnny Culloty to team-mate, Moss Keane, who made a 'slip up' in a game at the Kilkenny Beer Festival in 1972,* The Kerryman, *18 March 1988)*


His wit was a constant source of mirth in the dressing room. One of his remarks on a player he did not approve of was: 'He is so mean that if he was a ghost he wouldn't even give you a fright'.

*(Jo-Jo Barrett paying tribute to the late Gaffney Duggan, a well-known GAA 'bagman',* Kerry's Eye, *17 April 1974)*


He'll never make a good footballer; he suffers from duck's disease. His arse is too close to the ground.

*(Gaffney Duggan, former Kerry bagman, as related to Weeshie Fogarty, who related this to the author)*


There are a lot of high balls to be caught yet in Croke Park.

*(Great Kerry midfielder and 1955 captain John Dowling on the decline in the art of fielding, as quoted by Con Houlihan in* More Than A Game*)*

In football terms he had about as much refinement as a broken bottle and whenever he pulled on a jersey he looked as endearing as a bulldog.

*(Owen McCrohan's description of Páidí Ó Sé, in Owen McCrohan's* Mick O'Dwyer: The Authorised Biography*)*

A part of him was shy, a lot of people didn't see that. He was most comfortable in his own environment but he also loved Dublin.

*(Máire Ó Sé describing her husband, in Donal Keenan's* Páidí: A Big Life*)*

Mick O'Dwyer is justifiably ranked as one of the greatest managers ever in the history of Gaelic football. To me, he is *the* greatest and he has the track record to prove it.

*(Jimmy Deenihan,* My Sporting Life*)*

There were two men-of-the-match today, Liam. Yourself and Seamus Moynihan.

*(Weeshie Fogarty's remark to Radio Kerry match commentator Liam Higgins following Kerry's All-Ireland final win over Mayo in September 2006. Liam was terminally ill with cancer, attached to a morphine pump and yet gave a remarkable match commentary)*

It is like looking down from Aghadoe and seeing the majesty of the mountains and the lakes, so beautiful is the scene here.

*(Weeshie Fogarty's Radio Kerry commentary at the final whistle of the 1997 All-Ireland final as the Kerry supporters invaded Croke Park)*


Fifteen austere young men of Kerry watch the green hills flash by as their train rumbles up to Dublin.

A monastery would be proud of them.

Bachelors all, they sit pensively – as if in meditation – now and then exchanging a nervous word or two. About football.

For these are 'the men behind O'Dwyer', Kerry's youngest ever All-Ireland team, quietly confident of wresting the Sam Maguire Cup from the upstart Dubs at Croke Park today.

Wine, women and song have played no part in the lives of these magnificently fit titans for the past ten weeks.

They're all between 19 and 26 but not one of them is even engaged and cigarettes they spurn as the vice of softies.

*(Jim Farrelly,* The Sunday Independent, *28 September 1975)*


My old friend Jackie Lyne had his own theory about Kerry's pre-eminence. 'With those bastards of mountains in front of us, and those hoors of lakes behind us, sure there's nothing to do but play football.'

*(Con Houlihan,* Evening Herald, *21 September 2003)*

People will say that we are great losers and all that. We are gracious in defeat but, deep down, Kerry people don't like to lose.

Being Kerry manager is probably the hardest job in the world because Kerry people, I'd say, are the roughest kind of f**king animals you could ever deal with.

And you can print that.

*(Páidí Ó Sé's summation of Kerry fans in an interview with Kevin Kimmage,* Sunday Independent, *5 January 2003)*

I'm after giving an oul' interview at home, and I'm a small bit worried about it.

*(Páidí to his nephew, Dara Ó Cinnéide, in Cape Town, where they had arrived on the day of publication of the controversial interview with Kevin Kimmage. Quoted in Donal Keenan's* Páidí: A Big Life*)*

They're going bananas in Kerry.

*(Call made by the* Irish Independent *office to Kevin Kimmage at home. Quoted in Donal Keenan's* Páidí: A Big Life*)*

Kerry supporters. What I meant in the article about the Kerry supporters is that they are very hard to please, always demanding the highest standards because they are very proud people.

From time to time, I unfortunately go about describing things the wrong way and I apologise to the people of Kerry if I have hurt, disturbed or upset them in any way.

*(Apology issued by Páidí Ó Sé through Raidió na Gaeltachta)*


Páidí was right. We're 'onimals'.

*(A Kerry fan overheard by myself at a Munster final in Fitzgerald Stadium)*


Just make sure you beat Cork first.

*(Charlie Haughey to Páidí Ó Sé before opening the footballer's Ventry bar on 25 July 1985)*


At the moment it is a well-kept international secret that the GAA is the best amateur sports organisation in the world. I want the world to see the standards we have achieved in Croke Park. I want the fans, mentors and players in international sports to be exposed to the wonders of Croke Park. I want them to share the pride I feel for it.

*(Páidí Ó Sé in 'Time to open Croker' by Padraig Kennelly,* Kerry's Eye, *14 October 2004)*

The true essence of Páidí Ó Sé was that he meant so much to so many in many, many different ways. He made his name on the GAA fields of Kerry and in Croke Park but his story transcended his heroic deeds with the pigskin.

He was the rogue with the smile who rubbed shoulders with many leaders of this country …

In short, he was a man that you would want in your corner. Above all though, he was a son of An Gaeltacht.

*('Editorial',* The Kerryman, *19 December 2012)*

There isn't a question or a shadow of doubt about it. At present, I feel this confining of Croke Park to Gaelic Games is a pure, sheer nonsense. 'Tis absolutely ridiculous to put it mildly. We're all Irish and we all have the spirit of the Irish. We all helped to put Croke Park where it is. Every one of us that played and got our hands and legs broken and our heads split several times.

*(Jackie Healy-Rae interviewed by Liam Fay in 'The Kingdom's Kingmaker',* Hot Press, *31 May 1995)*

Nobody did it better than Maurice Fitzgerald. The debate about whether or not he should have started can end here and now. He is still a front line player for Kerry, as he proved with a wonderfully intelligent contribution in the final twenty minutes.

Fitzgerald sees gaps where others see roadblocks and while

he may lack the speed and energy of some younger Kerry colleagues, his subtlety and poise more than compensate. Indeed, it is the perfect topping in an exciting Kerry attack.

*(*Irish Independent *report on the All-Ireland replay against Galway on 7 October 2000 – Maurice came on as a sub that day)*

What drove me? I didn't know. I always just played to win. I wanted medals, achievement, success. I wanted respect. Pure and simple. With me it was always pure but rarely that simple, and once I gave it some thought, the answer, or some kind of answer, was not far away.

*(Paul Galvin,* In My Own Words*)*

The Brosnans were born in a part of Dingle known as The Colony, a row of fishermen's cottages adjacent to Strand Street, and they went to sea at an early age and followed the mackerel shoals as far away as Galway and Dunmore East …

Kerry mothers were known to admonish their children with such exhortations as: Eat your porridge or you won't grow big and strong like Paddy Bawn …

He was a big, rugged, raw-boned man who was as tough as any conger eel that ever swam in Dingle Bay. His deeds of gallantry on the football field were the stuff of legend …

He had neither the time nor the inclination for rigorous training pursuits.

In fact, he was once quoted as saying that the only training he needed for football was a few days on dry land to stretch his legs.

*(Owen McCrohan, 'Paddy Bawn Brosnan: his deeds of gallantry were the stuff of legend',* The Kerryman, *28 July 1995)*

Kerry were the poets but prose has its own high virtues.

*(Con Houlihan on Kerry's defeat to Armagh in the 2002 All-Ireland final, in* More Than a Game*)*

Little towns that football had historically bypassed – Ardfert Kilmoyley, Crotta, Lixnaw, Bennettsbridge, Abbeydorney, Causeway, Ballyduff, and so on. Out in the north of the county, a little cluster of nine parishes sent out nine hurling teams. In the south of the county, hurling survived in patches – Kenmare, Killarney, and Kilgarvan being the noted centres of activity. They played their championships and kept their pride and passion burning quietly.

*(Tom Humphries,* Green Fields*)*

Anybody can catch a ball but to go and get it from a distance, it takes a lot of practice.

*(Mick O'Connell quoted in 'Mick O'Connell, A Football Legend',* The Kerryman, *18 February 2000)*

…there are no born footballers or born hurlers or born poets or whatever.

Some people are born with more talent than others in certain fields but that talent needs to be cultivated.

Mick O'Connell is an example to every young player in whatever code; he worked very hard to fruitify his talent.

When first I watched him play, he was already a lovely fielder but his kicking was wayward.

It remained so even when he was established in the county's senior team; in time the man's kicking – and with either foot – seemed the most natural activity in the world.

*(Con Houlihan, 'Mick O'Connell, A Football Legend',*
The Kerryman, *18 February 2000)*

Two tricks? What are they? Is it putting the ball in the net and the ball over the bar?

*(A Kerry football fan in the Abbey Tavern, Tralee, responds to RTÉ analyst Martin McHugh's statement in August 2014 that Colm 'Gooch' Cooper was a 'two-trick pony'. The fan's response was given to me by* Kerry's Eye *sports editor Jim O'Gorman)*

If I were asked to name my greatest football team of all time, I would select the Kerry four-in-a-row team of 1981 because, at that stage, it had reached a level of perfection and understanding that, in my opinion, was unrivalled before or since ... In reality, that team turned out to be the forbearers of a revolution in Gaelic football in terms of fitness, playing style and modernisation that changed the game forever.

*(Jimmy Deenihan,* My Sporting Life*)*


*Mick O'Connell rubbishing the story that he left the Sam Maguire behind in the Croke Park dressing rooms after an All Ireland:*

Ah I didn't. I didn't forget it. It wasn't my job to bring it home because that particular night, like any other match I played in Dublin, I came home that night. My thought was to be there at eight or nine o'clock the following morning.

I worked for the Western Union Cable. Why should I as one of thirty-three staff get specialist treatment there? Why shouldn't other men with families to support get time off as well? I had my weekend off. I rowed home that night. We won a match, the same as the game in Cahersiveen, Killarney or Tralee. The game in Dublin was a game of football to me. It was the same ball, the green field and no more about it ...

I don't know what motivates other people to play but I just played because I actually liked the challenge of the game and anything else was incidental from that: awards or rewards, whatever you like, was incidental ...

*(Mick O'Connell quoted in 'Mick O'Connell, A Football Legend',*
The Kerryman, *18 February 2000)*

My first day in Croke Park was 17 March 1992, when I was chosen as mascot for Dr Crokes GAA Club in the All-Ireland club football final. I was delighted to be selected and as any other kid would be, I was extremely excited. Not only was it an historic day for Dr Crokes, but two of my brothers were playing on the team. From that day on, it was my goal to play in Croke Park on All-Ireland Final Day …

Little did I know that in 2002 I would be playing for Kerry in an All-Ireland against Armagh in front of 80,000 fans.

*(Colm 'Gooch' Cooper in Valerie O'Sullivan's* I am of Kerry*)*

Joe Brolly told us the production line was finished in Kerry – well, Joe Brolly, what do you think of that?

*(Kieran Donaghy lays it on the line for the RTÉ analyst in Croke Park after Kerry's All-Ireland win on 21 September 2014. www.rte.ie/sport/gaa/football/2014)*

The grit and determination of getting stuck into it and throwing everything they have at it seems to be gone. I think the young generations are getting more afraid of getting hurt and injured. When we went into a game we didn't give a damn if we never again came out of it …

*(Jackie Healy-Rae in Donal Hickey's* The Mighty Healy-Rae*)*

At least I will have a free seat on Sunday, a good view and 40,000 less people abusing me.

*(Pat Spillane's reaction to being relegated to the substitutes' bench at the Munster final,* The Kerryman, *29 June 1990)*

I swear to God, my mother would be faster than most of those three fellas and she has a bit of arthritis in the knee.

*(Pat Spillane on the RTÉ halftime analysis of the 2002 All-Ireland Final in which Armagh went on to beat Kerry. He said the remark was made tongue-in-cheek in relation to the Armagh full-back line)*

We could receive television in our neck of the woods and bogs by the time Moss Keane got his first cap. My father, God rest him, took a half-day from the creamery. He said, 'It would be a bad time for a man's horse to fall into a drain.'

The workplaces were deserted; by three o'clock there wasn't a dog on the streets. Moss' parents had never seen a rugby game. They bought a [TV] set for the match. We were playing France in Paris. The early exchanges were hectic. His mother said, 'I'm terrified that the young lad will break a leg.'

'He might,' said his father, 'but it won't be his own.'

*(Con Houlihan, 'In the Heat of Battle', in* In So Many Words: The Best of Con Houlihan*)*

Maurice Ignatius Keane. 18 and half stone of prime Irish beef on the hoof, I don't know about the opposition but he frightens the living daylights out of me.

*(Rugby commentator Bill McLaren, as quoted on www.telegraph. co.uk/sport/rugbyunion/international/ireland, 5 October 2010)*


Moss, you are no longer an experiment, you are a Munster man picked to play against the All Blacks. Just go out there and cause mayhem. Disrupt their line-out. Stop them getting quick ball. Stand up for yourself and your team. Kerrymen have won more All-Ireland finals than anybody else, you are afraid of nobody. Kerry are the All Blacks of Ireland. That's why we picked you.

*(Munster selectors' chairman Noel Murphy before Moss Keane's debut against the All Blacks in 1973.* Moss Keane, Rucks, Mauls & Gaelic Football*)*


England and Lions player Peter Wheeler recalled being invited to stay with Keane in Kerry. 'I flew in to Dublin and then caught a train. Moss was going to meet me at the station, but was not there. It was late at night and I managed to find his house. A woman answered the door and when I asked if Moss Keane lived there, she replied: 'Yes. Bring him in.'

*(*Moss Keane, Rucks, Mauls & Gaelic Football*)*

I thought it would be handy if someone had a bucket so we could make a few black puddings.

> *(Moss Keane on why he was laughing despite a gushing head wound playing for Ireland against France, in* Rucks, Mauls & Gaelic Football*)*

Beaumont, captain of a star-studded English side, approached Keane and said, 'May the best team win.' Keane, recognising the calibre of his opponents, replied, 'I hope they don't.'

> *(Moss Keane,* Rucks, Mauls & Gaelic Football*)*

In Munster's legendary 1978 defeat of the All Blacks, a frustrated Andy Haden started to swing a punch. Moss caught his arm and said, 'Don't. Ye will only lose the fight as well.'

> *(Moss Keane,* Rucks, Mauls & Gaelic Football*)*

Junior rugby in Kerry is like pornography – very frustrating to watch but maybe entertaining enough if you are actually involved.

> *(Moss Keane,* Rucks, Mauls & Gaelic Football*)*

Rugby has been my life. There's nothing fair about it. I have played with and against several players who deserved to be capped and never were. Lady luck and the hand of God play a huge part in all our lives. I think of my father who died at forty-eight and never saw me in a red or green jersey. I look at my family and know how much he would have adored them.

*(Mick Galwey in Valerie O'Sullivan's* I am of Kerry*)*


Spring's international [rugby] experience was blighted by one incident in 1979 which has gone down in folklore. He dropped a high ball near the Irish line in Cardiff Arms Park and Wales scored a try …

Dropping the ball was a psychological blow which stayed with Spring for a long time. 'Dick has a good sense of humour but you didn't make jokes about dropping the ball for a good few years afterwards,' says a friend.

Even at the Labour Conference of 1993, when party chairman, Jim Kemmy, made a crack about the dropped ball while introducing his leader before the keynote address, Spring put aside his speech for a moment to respond: 'I have always said that I will take criticism on that point from anybody who has played rugby for Ireland and hurling and football for Kerry, but I doubt if there is anybody else who has,' he said, before delivering his prepared speech on live television.

*(Stephen Collins,* Spring and the Labour Story*)*


I astonished a good many there with the length of my drive; they all wondered why a priest should play so well, for in this country they think a priest should live, eat, pray, sleep and die in the church and he is good for nothing else … The links are far from the City and besides, to be a member one must know how to rob a bank and to keep what is robbed.

*(Monsignor Hugh O'Flaherty in Brian Fleming's*
*The Vatican Pimpernel)*


Nothing like golf for knocking the troubles of this poor world out of your mind.

*(Monsignor Hugh O'Flaherty in Brian Fleming's*
*The Vatican Pimpernel)*


Even the priests in Killarney call me Killer.

*(Colourful Killarney character and former boxer John 'Killer' O'Callaghan, who had no objection to the name given to him during his glory days in the ring and afterwards, as related to the author by John O'Mahony)*


And of course, the proliferation of soccer in this island is about the best thing that happened to us since the arrival of the potato.

*(Con Houlihan, 'Football Mania – a global affliction', in* Windfalls*)*

People were gone 'clane mad' in the estimation of the man with the cap who saw the Poets Inn, Castleisland, erupt in jubilation all around him as Kevin Sheedy scored Ireland's first penalty.

'There isn't much sense to it,' he confided, shaking his head. 'They're all gone mad you know. People are gone clane mad.'

The wild cheers for Sheedy's goal appalled him. 'Will ye shet up,' he groaned.

Still, the magic of the World Cup ropes in the most unlikely fans and even he succumbed finally. David O'Leary had scored, the Poets Inn was a dancing, shouting, jumping minor Mardi Gras and he was in there with the best of them shouting, 'Up Kerry!'

*(Breda Joy, 'World Cup Mania in Kerry', The Kerryman, 29 June 1990)*

For as long as I can remember there has been a broadcasting box at the back of the Fitzgerald Stadium terrace and its location may hold the key to why Killarney is my favourite venue. The view from there at any time of year is breathtaking, with a long sweep of mountains taking in Corrán Tuathail, Ireland's highest peak, Mangerton, the Paps of Danann, and the many glens, ravines and folds of forest that have garnered world fame for Beauty's Home.

*(Micheál Ó Muircheartaigh, From Borroloola to Mangerton Mountain)*

I led the parade because Red Rum was number one on the card. I went down and showed him the first fence. And as it was a cold, dry April day, I got a rug put over his loins down at the start to keep him warm. The ground was drying up fast and that suited. It's like with athletes, the longer you can keep a horse warm the better. He was on his toes and he was wound up. Whatever feeling he got at Liverpool, you knew he sensed the place. He was like a coil underneath you about to explode. Yet he was not jumping or jigging, but on his toes …

That night we went back to Southport to a local hotel. I don't drink but everybody was drinking. Then they brought the horse into the hotel at about eleven o'clock. It was unbelievable. I will never forget it … they brought the horse into the ballroom and everyone was patting him.

*(Tommy Stack on riding Red Rum to the horse's third Aintree Grand National win in 1977, in Jimmy Woulfe's* Voices of Kerry*)*

When the horses had all run, a jennet race was held, and greatly delighted the people, as the jennets – there was a number of them – got scared by the cheering and ran wild in every direction. In the end it was not easy to say which was the winner, and a dispute began which nearly ended in blows. It was decided at last to run the race over again the following Sunday after Mass, so everyone was satisfied.

*(J. M. Synge describing the Glenbeigh Races, in* John M. Synge in West Kerry*)*

Raw foods are best – meat, eggs, cheese, vegetables, honey – and I always took quantities of cows' blood when I felt it was needed.

*(Cahersiveen Iron Man Mick Murphy, who won the 1958 Rás Tailteann, told Micheál Ó Muircheartaigh he always carried a penknife and knew how to extract blood from a cow's vein without causing any damage. Micheál Ó Muircheartaigh,*
From Borroloola to Mangerton Mountain*)*

The Iron Man disregarded established etiquette, rode solo away from the bunch and arrived in Kilkenny on his own. It was a performance that left the Rás astonished. The race leader's yellow jersey was then his. Legend tells that he then rode off that evening wearing the Yellow Jersey, did a thirty-mile training spin, stopped at a stone wall and with selected stones 'did weights' for an hour before drawing blood from a cow and returning to base. It is believed he did the transfusion three times during the Rás.

*(Tom Daly, 'The Rás', in Micheál Ó Muircheartaigh's*
From Borroloola to Mangerton Mountain*)*

I believed in striking to the front any chance I got and defied others to beat me.

*(Mick Murphy in Micheál Ó Muircheartaigh's*
From Borroloola to Mangerton Mountain*)*

A little to the west of The Slate House you may come across a grand young man driving in his cows or tending to his sheep.

His name is John Lenihan; his record as a runner on the roads and in cross country and on the hills can truly be described as fabulous.

He is a legendary hill runner; long ago he should have ridden in triumph from Dublin Airport in an open-topped bus with Jimmy Magee beaming on all and sundry (whoever they are) but our John has a genius for stealing home from the continent and elsewhere.

*(Con Houlihan, 'Journey back to the Kingdom's Heart', in* Windfalls*)*

*Asides in the match commentaries of Micheál Ó Muircheartaigh:*

Colin Corkery on the 45 lets go with the right boot. It's over the bar. This man shouldn't be playing football. He's made an almost Lazarus-like recovery from a heart condition. Lazarus was a great man but he couldn't kick points like Colin Corkery.

Seán Óg Ó Hailpín – his father's from Fermanagh, his mother's from Fiji, neither a hurling stronghold.

Teddy McCarthy to John McCarthy, no relation, John McCarthy to Teddy McCarthy, still no relation. Teddy looks at the ball – the ball looks at Teddy.

And Brian Dooher is down injured. And while he is, I'll tell ye a little story. I was in Times Square in New York last week, and I was missing the Championship back home. So I approached a news stand and I said, 'I suppose ye wouldn't have the Kerryman, would ye?' To which the Egyptian behind the counter turned to me and he said, 'Do you want the North Kerry edition or the South Kerry edition?' He had both – so I bought both. And Dooher is back on his feet.

*Asides in television match analyses of Pat Spillane on* The Sunday Game:

You get more contact in an old-time waltz at the old-folks' home than in a National League final.

The first half was even, the second half was even worse.

They have a forward line that couldn't punch holes in a paper bag.

*From Daniel O'Connell's letters:*

We have just come in from hunting and killing in high style a brace of hares. (*September 1834*)

I have had great hunting – only one blank day. I have, since I saw you, killed 77 hares. Yesterday the most splendid hunting I ever saw. (*To his son, John, from Derrynane, December 1840*)

The English only breed their dogs for speed, so that a fox-hunt becomes little more than a mere greyhound chase. I am the only fellow who understands how to hunt rationally – the instinct of the beagle in tracking out the hare is beautifully developed in the Derrynane hunts.

*(Daniel O'Connell quoted by William J. Daunt,* Personal Recollections of the Late Daniel O'Connell, MP*)*

# THE DEMON DRINK

Here's my pledge: to take no pledge
From now, until I die.
Here's my toast: in hell to roast,
If I should ever try.

*(Joseph O'Connor,* Hostage to Fortune*)*

By eight o'clock it [the column] was in the safe hands of the Sports Editor, Tom O'Shea, and I was in my favourite corner in The White Horse – the corner nearest the quay. There I loved to read *The Sporting Life* and I sustained myself with a glass of milk mildly tinctured with brandy. So I had something in common with the Queen Mother: At eight every morning that same paper was brought to her bed accompanied by a large measure of gin and a bottle of tonic water.

*(Con Houlihan, 'My Dublin days of milk and brandy and papers past',* Independent.ie. *Published 16 January 2008)*

God help him he's cursed with an awful tooth for porter.

*(John B. Keane,* The Little Book of John B. Keane*)*

Drink follows music and, if you take my advice, stay away from the whiskey because it will put a shake in your hand and it will scatter your mind.

*(Musician Joe Cooley to Maidhc Dainín Ó Sé, in* House Don't Fall on Me*)*


A drunk man will get sober but a fool never gets sense.

*(A saying of Mick Kelly, Gullane, Gneeveguilla, a first cousin of Seanchaí Éamon Kelly, as related to the author by Tom Joe O'Donoghue, Gneeveguilla)*


Did you never hear the parish priest's sermon?

It's whisky makes you bate your wives; it's whisky makes your homes desolate; it's whisky makes you shoot your landlords, and' – with emphasis, as he thumped the pulpit – 'it's whisky makes you miss them.'

*(Samuel Hussey,* The Reminiscences of an Irish Land Agent*)*


Booze to the sober man is what flood waters are to the stranded fish, what the starting pistol is to the straining athlete, what the sound of the whistle is to the waiting midfielder.

*(John B. Keane,* The Little Book of John B. Keane*)*

Tim the Thirst.

> *(Nickname of a certain Kerryman with an 'awful tooth for porter',
> heard by the author in south Kerry)*

I even had a glass of Guinness which confirmed my suspicion that it really was liquid shoe polish.

> (*Maureen Erde*, Help! I'm an Irish Innkeeper)

Ned was noted, but fierce, for the drink. One of the pledges Ned took only allowed him one drink a day. He settled for a pint. That was all right until he was seen pouring two pints into a quart jug, making one drink of it. He went from the quart to the sweet gallon and finished up worse than ever …

> (*Éamon Kelly*, The Apprentice)

No man was born into this world with a more passionate love of liquor than myself. It's not just that I love liquor for the taste of it. I love the plop of whiskey into a glass. I love it. I love to listen to it. I love to see the cream on a pint. I love the first powerful, violent impact of a glass of whiskey when I throw it back on me and it hits me there below. I chase it then with a pint.

(*John B. Keane on drink*, YouTube, *uploaded on 13 February 2009*)

I could live for weeks and months without going into any pub. I was never a great drinker but there's people driving all my life with four or five pints … Go to the police and ask how many accidents were these people that I'm speaking about involved in. There were no bloody accidents. I never let a drunk man out of the pub. I'd lose my licence if I did. I often took the keys off a fella and let him walk in preference to see him drive. But if I asked a man with four pints or four and a half pints of Guinness in him for the keys of his car, he'd think I'd gone around the bend.

*(Jackie Healy-Rae's response to tougher drink driving laws introduced on 2 December 1994 by the then Minister for the Environment Michael Smith, in Liam Fay's 'The Kingdom's Kingmaker',* Hot Press, *31 May 1995)*

I should pause here and say that my usual drink is wine, and Irish bar wine is horrible, and the Irish system of ordering rounds is lethal for anyone who wants to cling on to any appearance of sobriety. So after a few sessions where, when it finally came to my turn to buy a round, and I was practically flat out on the bar, I devised a defensive Irish drinking routine. I would buy the first round and make my drink a bottle of rosé. This way I could easily pass on drinks when the following rounds were bought, and also leave whenever I wanted to with whatever was left of my bottle of wine.

*(Maureen Erde,* Help! I'm an Irish Innkeeper*)*

## THE DEMON DRINK

And your father has not come home yet. Drinking money that we could do with to hold house and home where he is the only wage-earner, while I run myself to rags to keep up appearances in ye. 'Tis at the point now that one week of idleness for him and disaster faces all my hopes.

*(Seamus de Faoite, 'The American Apples',
in* The More We Are Together*)*

Conservatively dated back to 1798, the premises and its ambience is breathing proof that television and such distractions have long outstayed their welcome in pub life today.

For it's here that people, who just want to talk or sing or be left alone, gather around the glow from the embers of the pub culture we knew and loved – and the porter there is among the best in town.

It is here too, for generations, that locals shared the news of the town and surrounding areas and sat until every angle was teased out. Then they ticked off their groceries, bagged them, threw down their half-ones, drank their mediums and made for the door with a barely audible 'Put them in the book.'

*(John Reidy, 'Sheila Prendiville's – Defying description at No. 22',*
The Kerryman, *21 October 2004)*

There were to be sports at noon in Ballyferriter, and when we had talked for a while I asked the host if he would think well of my going over to see them. 'I would not,' he said; 'you'd do better to stay quiet in this place where you are; the men will be all drunk coming back, fighting and kicking in the canoes, and a man, the likes of you, who aren't used to us, would be frightened. Then, if you went, the people would be taking you into one public-house, and then into another; till you'd maybe get drunk yourself, and that wouldn't be a nice thing for a gentleman. Stay where you are in this island and you'll be safest so …'

We went in again to the fire and spoke about porter and whisky (I have never heard the men here talk for half an hour of anything without some allusion to drink), discussing how much a man could drink with comfort in a day, whether it is better to drink when a man is thirsty or at ordinary times, and what food gives the best liking for porter.

*(J. M. Synge,* John M. Synge in West Kerry*)*


Patsy would sell his mother for a pint, but would wade through fire and water to carry out a promise he had given to get that pint. The bright boys of the town knew that and often played on it. They got him to kiss Minnie Lyons, the town beauty, coming out from the crowded twelve o'clock Mass on Easter Sunday, and bribed him with a quart of Guinness to welcome the Judge of Assizes on the Courthouse steps on the morning of a packed trial of political prisoners.

*(Joseph O'Connor,* Hostage to Fortune*)*

## The Demon Drink

It is not considered etiquette to come out of Killorglin sober on Puck Fair; and, judging by the state of the people in the vicinity in the evening, this social custom is rigidly observed.

*(Samuel Hussey,* The Reminiscences of an Irish Land Agent*)*


A gallon of fresh fiery whisky. A pint of rum. A pint of methylated spirit. Two ounces of corrosive sublimate. Three gallons of whisky.

*(Recipe for 'the special whisky for Puck Fair' as given by Samuel Hussey,* The Reminiscences of an Irish Land Agent*)*


Four men fought together in one place till the tide came up on them, and was likely to drown them; but the priest waded out up to his middle and drove them asunder. Another man was left for dead on the road outside the lodges, and some gentleman found him and had carried him into his house, and got the doctor to put plasters on his head. Then there was a red-headed fellow had his finger bitten through, and the postman was destroyed forever …

'It was this was the cause of it all,' said Danny-boy: 'they brought in porter east and west from the two towns you know of, and the two porters didn't agree together, and it's for that the people went raging at the fall of night.

*(J. M. Synge,* John M. Synge in West Kerry*)*

In my young days it was deemed an essential point of hospitality to make guests drink against their will – drink til they were sick. I was myself the first person who rebelled against this custom in Iveragh.

*(William J. Daunt*, Personal Recollections of the Late Daniel O'Connell, MP*)*

Serving behind the bar for the Fleadh Cheoil is an education. Each face that beckons you has a story to tell …

Of course, there is the exception that proves the rule; he breezes into the bar looking as sober as a judge, walks confidently to the counter and orders his drink. Once served he reverts back to his true state, that of advanced drunkenness. In this case, there is little you can do, only hope that he doesn't deposit his pint on the floor …

Jack Mulvihill, a native of Moyvane and a man who likes a pint or two gave me the following advice on trying to size up customers: 'If he's wearing a cap, he's sound as bell metal.' Michael Lynch of Affoula added: 'Divide everything you hear behind the bar by six …'

Another aspect of the festival is that it is usually the small, thin patron that is the most aggressive when drunk. The bigger and taller the man the mellower he is. The person who said that God made big men quiet must have worked behind the bar.

*(John Keane, 'Behind the bar at the Fleadh',* The Kerryman, *11 September 1987)*

# The Demon Drink

As I said, like most of us who have trodden the boards, he loved the Dark Queen – the porter that soothes some breasts, and brings the bleak gremlins of despair to others.

I, myself, am no stranger to bleak mornings and alcoholic remorse. When I first met Éamon Keane, my main hobby in life was black porter, Bendigo tobacco, and tall tales.

On the sauce or off the sauce Éamon's talent and generosity never wavered.

Other writers will write more deeply about Éamon Keane, his acting, and his stage craft in plays and one-man shows, and the two Jacob's awards he won. I am writing here and now about a man who was my friend. A man who walked through life, eyes always searching for the end of the rainbow. Sleep well Éamon!

*(Seán McCarthy, 'Searching for the End of the Rainbow',*
*The Kerryman, January 1990)*


One of the very few short-tempered letters in his [Daniel O'Connell's] vast correspondence was prompted by his disappointment at the poor quality of wines delivered:

I am much disappointed in many things. The wines I got from Cork are by no means satisfactory. Can you tell the quantity and nature of the wine you ordered? [...] I have got a wooden box containing 3 dozen bottles by Sir D. Roose. I have got besides 6 hampers of sherry containing 24 dozen or thereabouts. There are 4 hampers of Sauternes containing about

12 dozen altogether. The port is fair wine enough. Some of the sherry is very bad. The Sauternes appears also very indifferent. There is also a hamper marked to contain 6 dozen Madeira.

*(Probably August 1832, to John Primrose in Derrynane, quoted by Dr Grace Neville in her talk entitled 'Daniel O'Connell: Food, Feast and Famine')*


My father drinks too much that night. And he keeps drinking. Through days of remorse and promises, and nights, so many nights, of that voice filled with rage and pain. My father is being pulled further away from us.

*(Fergal Keane writing about his father, Éamon, in* All of These People*)*


When I was young this cousin used to go on skites a few times a year. When he would not be well, he would send word to my mother. My father would go over in the pony and trap and collect him, and he would spend six weeks in our house. And, strangely enough, in most of the alcohol treatment programmes, six weeks is the duration. My mother would dry him out by giving him a few bottles of stout each day. And then she would wean him off and when he would be rested and back in the full of his health he would go off home.

*(Sister Consilio in Jimmy Woulfe's* Voices of Kerry*)*

## The Demon Drink

In the summer of 1986, I spent two months trying to think about alcoholism. I walked from St Patrick's Hospital to Ballsbridge one Sunday and when I was walking, my mind told me to stop drinking. I wondered: 'Is being a lapsed alcoholic a form of betrayal?' I had to think about that ...

I like drunkards. I like drink. I don't like myself. I don't like being afraid of life. I am timid. I'm not shy any more. I love the pub for an hour or an hour and a half. The great thing is they are centres of transformation. People change after a few drinks. They drink articulately to another planet and you are left alone on yours.

*(Brendan Kennelly interviewed by Justine McCarthy fifteen years after he had stopped drinking, 'The Keeper of the Spirit',* Irish Independent, *4 July 2001)*

It is possible that stories of Paddy Bawn's drinking exploits have been greatly exaggerated but, at any rate, his cure for a hangover deserves to be preserved for posterity. Any sufferer who might have imbibed not wisely but too well was advised to drink the 'soup' of a few boiled cod first thing in the morning. Not for the faint-hearted.

*(Owen McCrohan, 'Paddy Bawn Brosnan: his deeds of gallantry were the stuff of legend',* The Kerryman, *28 July 1995)*

The bar was dark, with a low ceiling and only a small window to allow in the light. We were well known in that house. My grandfather, on his way from town, was a regular customer there. The pony that pulled his tub trap stopped at John Dan's of her own accord.

*(Éamon Kelly,* The Apprentice*)*


There never was an outrage committed without an empty whisky bottle being found close to the scene of the murder.

*(Samuel Hussey,* The Reminiscences of an Irish Land Agent*)*

# CHRISTMAS

Taken in good measure Christmas is the best of all known antidotes for bitterness.

*(John B. Keane,* The Little Book of John B. Keane*)*

Miserable, grey mist, moulded into large blobs, like overweight dragoons riding ghostly steeds, swirled around St John's Church. The town of Tralee, that in a few days time would be aglow with Christmas lights, squatted, damp and lonely now – a bride waiting for her new gown …

The open log fire in Benner's Hotel was a sight to warm the heart of an Eskimo with the 'flu.

*(Seán McCarthy, 'Encounter by the log fire in Benners Hotel',*
The Kerryman, *5 January 1990)*

Every Christmas, the children set themselves the task of saying 4,000 'Hail Marys' between the first day of December and Christmas Eve. The figure was taken to correspond with the 4,000 years spent waiting for the birth of Jesus.

Christmas was a simple affair then: the house was decorated with moss to keep the infant Jesus from 'hurting his toes', and holly and ivy were entwined around the windows.

The Christmas candle was bedded in a jam crock of sand and flowers were made out of paper.

*(Monsignor Pádraig Ó Fiannachta,* The Kerryman, *12 June 1998)*


The Wren, the wren the king of all birds,
St Stephen's Day he was caught in the furze,
Up with the kettle and down with the pan,
A penny or two to bury the wren.

*(Verse sung by the Kerry 'Wren Boys', also known as the 'Wran Boys', who parade and play music on St Stephen's Day or the 'Wran's Day')*


It's a Christmas story you couldn't make up. Visitors to Saint Mary's Cathedral in Killarney this week were enjoying bursts of heavenly birdsong – courtesy of a living, breathing robin who has taken up residence in the Cathedral's Christmas crib.

During the anniversary Mass of local teenager, Nathan O'Carroll on Friday, vocalists found themselves facing stiff competition as the new resident made his heavenly presence heard. The bird also takes regular flights around the church before heading back to the crib.

*('Robin tweets from Cathedral's crib',* Kerry's Eye, *23 December 2014)*

If there was just one thing to commend the early fall of darkness in winter, it would have to be that very special glow that shines through the streets in Killarney at Christmas time.

As the natural light ebbs away over the rooflines into the arms of the evening, the window displays brighten and the Christmas lights arch the streets in garlands of colour …

Christmas in Killarney is about a sense of belonging. It is a season for coming home and being with the people cut from the same cloth as yourself …

Christmas in Killarney is about missing the characters, the family members and the friends who are no longer here to share the joys of the season. It is about raising a glass to their memory and being thankful that they walked the road with us.

*(Breda Joy, 'Christmas time in Killarney', The Kerryman, 3 December 1993)*

When darkness fell on Christmas Eve the youngest child in the house lit the first candle, my father's large hand making the sign of the cross on his small head and shoulders. The other candles were lit from this and we raced from room to room revelling in the new blaze of light, and out into the yard to see what the effect was like from outside. We watched the bunches of lights come on in the houses of the townland. They were like clusters of stars as they appeared down the valley and up the rising ground to Rossacrue …

It was time now for my mother to open the Christmas box

she got in Reidy's shop when we dealt in town. There was a bottle of wine for herself. That was put away to share with the women who called on small Christmas night, the women's Christmas (6 January).

My father would never look at the Christmas cake. His eye was on the big brown jar full of porter and resting on top of the bin. He wouldn't drink unless he had company. Knowing this, my mother sent me for our next door neighbour to come and sit with us.

*(Éamon Kelly,* The Apprentice*)*

West Kerry's Wrens trounced the bad weather which set in over the south-west on Stephen's Day. By nightfall the storm had been sent spinning northwards, and the quiet of a calm December evening was broken only by the sound of Wrens celebrating in all corners of the countryside.

In Dingle the Green and Gold were the first into the eye of the storm, quickly followed – or at any rate, followed by the Goat Street and Sráid Eoin. With the wind gusting to 70 miles an hour, the Sráid Eoin Wren had hardly reached the bottom of John Street when the poles carrying the banner snapped under the strain.

The two young Rohans carrying the banner picked up what remained and carried on up Main Street.

The wind-tunnels created by the curve of a street or a bend on the road sent straw men, hobby horses and wrenboys flying, and the banner-bearers looked for all the world as if they were hang-gliding, but the turbulence was faced head on by men and women well used to rolling with the swings and roundabouts of a Wren's Day. Only at one point did the wind hold sway, when the salt spray whipped by the gale blocked progress beyond the quay.

*(Peter Malone, 'Wren boys play havoc with the bad weather as the high winds and rain lash Dingle',* The Kerryman, *1 January 1999)*


Listowel was good to Éamon Kelly. He arrived in town as a Woodwork Teacher and left as an actor, broadcaster, storyteller and seanchaí, having married a wonderful actress, our own Maura O'Sullivan, in 1951.

However, my personal memories of Éamon Kelly are from when I was a small boy of 4 or 5 years of age. It was a few days before Christmas and excitement was running high in our house. One night before Éamon went home on holidays I was in bed when my father called me down to the sitting room.

As I squatted before the fire with my brothers my father asked Éamon to 'try out one of your stories on them'. Éamon spread his fingers and began – 'In my father's time …' We were speechless and spellbound hanging on the master storyteller's every word. The rest is history.

Later that week, my father told me to call to our neighbour, Eileen Moran, as there was a surprise for me. Eileen was my godmother. Can you imagine my joy and excitement on discovering that the present was a beautiful handcrafted wooden model garage with my own name engraved thereon? It had been crafted by my other godparent, Éamon Kelly, and was a treasured possession for many years.

*(Owen MacMahon,* The Kerryman, *19 November 1999)*

Christmas was our great festival. About two or three weeks before Christmas, there was often what we called The Christmas East Wind, a period of calm seas. At that time the men would row the long journey to Dingle for the Christmas stores. At other times they had to go through Dún Chaoin ...

There was no holly on the island, it was as bare as my palm, no tree would grow on its windswept slopes. But there was lots of ivy, and we pulled quantities of that.

Candles were packed in jam jars, and one was put in every window of every house. This was the only time of year when there was light anywhere other than the kitchen ...

Christmas was a great time to get a parcel from America, or a letter with dollars ... I think it was at that time that I heard of Chickopea Falls. I thought it a strange and wonderful name. Many years later, in the States myself, I saw the sign, and for old times' sake, I had to make a detour to see the town I had dreamed so much about in my childhood.

*(Máirín Ní Dhuinnshléibhe, Bean Uí Bheoláin, in Brenda Ní Shúilleabháin's* Bibeanna: Memories from a Corner of Ireland*)*

We had never had a Christmas tree at home. A large candle left alight all night was one of the customs in Kerry and we had one in the kitchen window. Seen in cottage windows on a mountain-side these candles looked particularly attractive and reminded one of the simple faith of the people. The reason for these candles is in case the 'Holy Family' should pass, the light would guide them to a home and shelter.

*(Bertha Beatty,* Kerry Memories*)*

The Captain's skin and clipped beard, with their look of hoar frost and berries, gave him the cut of a superior Santa Claus in baggy tweeds.

*(Seamus de Faoite, 'Sky is Plentiful',*
*in* The More We Are Together*)*

# A WAY WITH WORDS

One wonders in these places why anyone is left in Dublin, or London, or Paris, when it would be better, one would think, to live in a tent or hut with this magnificent sea and sky, and to breathe this wonderful air, which is like wine in one's teeth.

*(J. M. Synge,* John M. Synge in West Kerry*)*


The harmless little squiggle called the apostrophe has almost broken up marriages and caused trouble among families. It is so simple that people cannot accept it – they become mesmerised. It is my belief that anybody who misuses the apostrophe is capable of anything.

*(Con Houlihan, 'Con Houlihan: Avoiding a spell of trouble',* Herald.ie, *15 June 2011)*


It was a small, neat house with walls fresh as white milk and laced by wires anchored to heavy stones to keep the thatch from flying over the mountain when the great winds blew from the sea.

*(Sigerson Clifford, 'The Spanish Waistcoat', in* Irish Short Stories*)*

He was extremely thin and his clothes hung loosely about him as though someone had pitched them carelessly upon him with a hayfork ...

The bullock was also very thin. He was a black yearling with the brown patient eyes of his kind ... He was like a slim upturned canvas-canoe on legs ...

His brother had sold four heifers while you'd be cracking an egg. Fifteen pounds a skull he got for them ...

They both had tongues as sharp as a cobbler's awl ...

She was a stout roomy woman with blue patches like maps on the calves of her legs ...

He had the loud, fat laugh of a man who always eats a good meal and has a roll of notes in his inside pocket to pay for it.

*(Sigerson Clifford, 'The Red-Haired Woman', in* Irish Short Stories*)*


I was born in a blizzard. I'm a Sagittarius, a hunter of fish and animals. I'm not a settled person. Man the Hunter, a hunter of the image. I'm a hunter of words.

If you are a writer, you are a hunter. You're looking for ideas and words. If you sit back and stop hunting, you're finished.

*(Con Houlihan,* The Kerryman, *19 June 1998)*


Do you no mydell?

*(Cant or Gammon language used by Travellers and meaning,*
*'Do you know who I am?')*

It was a lovely sight, praise on high to God, who made heaven and earth, and I fell to thinking of all the happy days I had spent in view of those hills and recalled the words of my grandfather: Twenty years a-growing, twenty years in bloom, twenty years a-stooping, and twenty years declining.

*(Maurice O'Sullivan,* Twenty Years A-Growing*)*


The walls were the most grotesque shade of green I had ever seen. As a nurse I had seen better colours coming out of patients' naso-gastric tubes.

*(Maureen Erde,* Help! I'm an Irish Innkeeper*)*


Oh, the best of all livings … the fruit of the earth … the growth of the animal … the pride of possession … a part of your country that you can make the greenest part of all Ireland. You can hate it sometimes but you can love it always.

*(Cahersiveen playwright, Pauline Maguire,* The Last Move. *Courtesy of the Maguire family archive)*


Wisha, 'tis better than being in the slush – same old thing every day – this an ugly spot, and the people ignorant, grumpy, and savage.

*(Kerry playwright George Fitzmaurice, 'The Magic Glasses',* The Plays of George Fitzmaurice*)*

That would be nothing to compare with having this place here, that's bred in your blood. And when yourself is left without land you'll be as common as the thousands, with only the bank book to back your name ... if you gave it a chance here, and let yourself find your roots here. For there's nothing in the world to beat the satisfaction of owning land.

*(From* Green Dust, *a play by Pauline Maguire, accepted by the Abbey in 1957 but never staged. Courtesy of the Maguire family archive)*

Speaking in the company of other Gaelic speakers in west Kerry I'd feel very uninhibited. My pronunciation in English is a bit suspect, but not so in Gaelic. English is a funny language, but I love it, of course. I grew up speaking Hiberno-English: English woven on a Gaelic loom.

*(Con Houlihan in Con Houlihan's Ireland – The Lost Essays,*
Irish Independent, *9 March 2013)*

The hands closed over my young pigeon in a way that would not have spoilt the wing-dust of a moth.

*(Seamus de Faoite, 'Sky is Plentiful',
in* The More We Are Together*)*

For many years I looked through the big school window at the world outside and saw many things. On a winter morning I looked out over the river on a rising frosty bogland, covered in whirls of white mist shot with rays of bright winter sun. A tall man strode through the scene, and his dogs moved back and forth around him. He looked like a wraith moving through a heavenly place, and I longed to be with him and to travel with him in freedom, to whatever land he was striding towards.

*(Rory O'Connor,* Gander at the Gate*)*


Author is prepared to sell outright all rights in 14 plays dealing intimately with life in the Irish countryside. Most have been either produced or published, suitable to which to build musical, television, etc. pass to anyone interested.

*(Note found in the belongings of playwright George Fitzmaurice (1877–1963) in Harcourt Street, Dublin, after his death, and rediscovered by Dr Fiona Brennan, in* George Fitzmaurice: 'Wild in His Own Way'*)*


Then the cliff breaks to the sea, and three miles out lie the islands. They are the peaks of hills sundered from their mainland brothers, and seen thus from above you would think them sea-monsters of an antique world languidly lifting time-worn backs above the restless and transitory waters.

*(Robin Flower describing the Blaskets in* The Western Island*)*

She spread herself all over the company like a hen preparing to hatch.

*(John B. Keane,* The Little Book of John B. Keane*)*


Renagown was – and presumably still is – about seven miles from my ancestral home; I used to travel there on my trusty bike with the lowslung handlebars; I felt like Stephen Roche before he was born. The last three miles are downhill; I flowed along by the infant Smearla; the fusion of spokesong and streamsong made lovely music.

*(Con Houlihan, 'Renagown NS – Higher Education in a Magic Land', in* Windfalls*)*


And the hedges are blessed with the pale pink and white of the flowering currant.

It surprises and delights me that such a delicate plant can flourish in those unlikely surroundings; it is rather as if you saw Princess Diana dancing a set at Puck Fair.

*(Con Houlihan, 'Journey back to the Kingdom's heart', in* Windfalls*)*


In togs she had a large white belly like a harvest frog.

*(John B. Keane,* The Little Book of John B. Keane*)*

In his speech he gave a lively description of a hunt among the Derrynane mountains, and of the effect produced by the music of the hounds among the wild glens of Iveragh. 'The very rocks,' said he, 'seem animated – they are vocal with their thousand answering echoes.'

*(William J. Daunt,* Personal Reflections of the Late Daniel O'Connell, MP*)*


The elements are the mentors of Kerrymen. They can patter like rain, roar like thunder, foam like the sea, sting like frost, sigh like the wind and on top of all that you'll never hear them boasting.

*(John B. Keane,* The Little Book of John B. Keane*)*


The sun was just setting and the western sky was as luminous and colourful as mother of pearl; the sea was utterly still and lay before us like a great mirror in which all this opulent beauty was given to us in two-fold measure; a few late birds moved noiselessly across the exquisite velvet of the eastern heavens; and then a great moon arose, big as a balloon and yellow as wild honey, and threw a shimmering causeway of light across the wide bay.

*(Richard Hayward describing the view from Waterville's seafront, in* In the Kingdom of Kerry*)*

Your theological rantings have the same effect on the people of Listowel as the droppings of an underfed blackbird on the water levels of the Grand Coulee dam.

*(John B. Keane,* The Little Book of John B. Keane*)*

Ballycarberry Castle and Caher Geal stood out clearly in the golden light, Doulus Head was a dream of tawny purple, and all the mountains above and beyond Caherciveen slumbered in a gentle haze that was gathering with the setting sun.

*(Richard Hayward describing the view from Knightstown on Valentia Island, in* In the Kingdom of Kerry*)*

Here, ordinary speech is frowned upon. Listening to the farmers on a fair day, you'd think it was Irish. What's spoken here is the love-child of Elizabethan England and Bardic Irish.

*(John B. Keane interviewed by Colm Toibin in the Iarnród Éireann magazine,* On Board, *c. 1990)*

The bishop has the cuteness of a pet fox and the long distance eye of a starving gannet.

*(John B. Keane, 'Letters of a Successful TD', in* Celebrated Letters of John B. Keane, *Vol. 1)*

It is better that our stories be recorded than they end up in the graveyard in Cill Chuáin.

*(Bríd Bean Uí Mhuircheartaigh in Brenda Ní Shúilleabháin's* Bibeanna: Memories from a Corner of Ireland)

There's a book in everyone. It's not always necessary to publish it and if you can't write it yourself you should let it be drawn out of you by somebody. Afterwards the world will have a fuller understanding of you and many things about you will be explained in a way that is not possible by expiring silently with the whole secret of your life locked up within you …

*(John B. Keane,* The Little Book of John B. Keane)

'We love kicking the shit out of each other,' says the professor of modern literature. 'I think I've got some unfair criticism. I think in Ireland what we do is label each other. The label of the Kerryman, the Trinity College professor, the jovial person, the "good old Brendan Kennelly" figure, and then they bring these to bear on what you write. I don't expect warm criticism. George Moore said a good literary movement is a number of people in a city with a cordial hatred for each other.'

*(Justine McCarthy, 'Keeper of the Flame',* Irish Independent, *4 July 2001)*

Usually I worked the column out in my head during the night – occasionally in some congenial pub – and got up at about four in the morning and wrote it.

*(Con Houlihan, 'My Dublin days of milk and brandy and papers past', Independent.ie, 16 January 2008)*


Nobody commanded the pages of the Irish newspapers quite like Con Houlihan. He was equal parts humility and insight. He wrote with the swerve of a poet, but in great big gambolling leaps.

When I first got to know him, he wrote in the sports pages of the *Evening Press* and on Wednesdays he wrote a literary column that my father, Seán McCann, edited. I loved to read whatever Con wrote. The evening was made wider by him. He could give a greyhound immediate muscle. He could put a swerve on a Liam Brady free kick. He could jockey us into the saddle when the rain was coming down over Aintree. He could make the turf at Lansdowne Road slide under your studs.

*(Colum McCann in Con Houlihan's Ireland – The Lost Essays, Irish Independent, 2 March 2013)*


Con, you gave me my third-level education.

*(A line from a letter to Con from a grateful Dublin fan, 'Foreword', in* Windfalls*)*

[He] wouldn't give you the dirt under his toe-nails if he thought 'twould do you any good.

*(John B. Keane,* The Little Book of John B. Keane*)*


The sun bedded down red into the west beyond the tree and the crown of leaves was like a brazier.

*(Seamus de Faoite, 'Sky is Plentiful',
in* The More We Are Together*)*


Considering the play's folk origins, the raw and brutal theme and the daring melodrama of its language, the Abbey's rejection of it was more a reflection of a bankrupt artistic policy than on the work itself.

*(Joe Dowling referring to John B. Keane's* Sive
*in* The Irish Times, *21 November 1992)*


A shrub with flowers the colour of orange peel has blossomed at the top of the hill before the house. Down in the gardens, one grand old rhododendron dame has rouged her cheeks with scarlet blossoms. Her companions bear green buds closed tightly as a baby's fist.

Perfumed freesias and hyacinths are flowering in the shelter of the limestone rockery where the rich bed of earth tells of the invisible care that nurtures their growth.

A few miniature purple bells have bloomed on an 'ugly duckling' shrub which will be transformed completely in another few weeks. Miniature green leaves, just out of their protective covering, are poised as delicately as ballerinas on a young tree by the stream. New growth is appearing too in the bed of 'giant rhubarb' which had withered into the ground for the winter.

Only a few daffodils had put their heads out under the copper beech three weeks back. Now a complete lemon-yellow halo rings the base of the tree. In the woodland behind the deer fence lipstick-red camelias are blooming …

While it's most pleasurable to see spring taking hold out in Muckross, the signs of change are in the town as well.

Counihan's horses are being brought in from the country to have their winter coats groomed in preparation for the season. Jaunting cars are lining out down the block.

Soon it will be time for the swallows and the Yanks!

*(Breda Joy, 'Spring is in the air at Muckross',*
*The Kerryman, 25 March 1988)*


In a rumble of iron-shod wheels Mick Breen's dray lantern rocked down the lane like a buoy-light in an inshore harbour. The shoes of his Clydesdale chipped flint sparks big as matchspurts off the cobbles.

*(Seamus de Faoite, 'The American Apples',*
*in* The More We Are Together*)*

Taking both my hands in his, he said, 'Yesterday, your face was a snowflake, Annie, and now your cheeks are as red as votive lamps.'

*(Bishop Eamonn Casey to Annie Murphy,* Forbidden Fruit*)*


'You couldn't have luck,' she teased him. 'And foxy women as plentiful as crows in the land.'

She was a tall, splendidly built woman with cruel blue eyes.

*(Sigerson Clifford, 'The Red-Haired Woman',*
*in* Irish Short Stories*)*


Books provided me with the consolation that the nuns failed to. I became totally preoccupied with them and escaped between their covers whenever I could.

Books offered me the possibility of a new and better tomorrow.

*(Michael Clemenger,* Holy Terrors. A Boy. Two Brothers.
A Stolen Childhood*)*


For I am a land agent by profession and an anecdotist only by habit.

*(Samuel Hussey,* The Reminiscences of an Irish Land Agent*)*

# SEX, MARRIAGE AND OTHER SHENANIGANS

When you marry a Kerry woman, you're kind of married to the county.

*(Cork-born Bill Murphy on his retirement as garda inspector in Killarney,* The Kerryman, *12 January 1990)*

Kerry's own Mary Lucey strode on stage with a confident wave of her hand. Asked about her two favourite politicians, she launched into a colourful account of a chance meeting with An Taoiseach at last year's festival (Rose of Tralee).

Asked by a bouncer to get off the car she was sitting on, she turned around to see Charlie Haughey sitting inside it.

'He asked me would I like to go for a (pause) drive,' she laughed, 'but my mother pulled me back. She said Charlie's a bit gamey.'

*(*The Kerryman, *26 August 1988)*

Love is a thing that torment and torture follows and often it's not lasting, and it's a small thing that upsets it.

*(Peig Sayers,* An Old Woman's Reflections*)*

To me getting on with women is a logical extension of how I played football. That is devilment, doing my best, but always having a sense of humour about the outcome and enjoying the company of the fellow I was marking, even when he was dirty.

Once you get to know a woman's mind, her feelings, her perspective on experience, you are into a different county altogether. And let the sexuality pour through all that experience. Sexuality should not be confined to copulation. It should run through education, religion, saying prayers. The oldest poets used to say prayers to the saints which were sexual. They expressed their whole beings. God didn't give you a being to be ashamed of.

*(Brendan Kennelly in Jimmy Woulfe's* Voices of Kerry*)*


I learned that the shelter of a bush with two people is better than a palace with three.

*(The Hiker in* The Year of the Hiker *by John B. Keane)*


A tailor he was, and he had a big beard and two wives, and men with beards and two voyages into marriage were rare enough in the town in those days anyway.

*(Sigerson Clifford, 'My South Kerry Grandfathers',*
*in* Irish Short Stories*)*

She dressed a thorny bed for herself.

*(Mike in* Sive *by John B. Keane)*


A young man confided in him one night a few years ago that he was going out with a woman a 'good bit older' than him and wondered what Dauber thought of it.

'Aisy Pati,' said Dauber, ''tisn't for racing you want her' came the reply from the impromptu agony aunt.

*(John Reidy, 'Sheila Prendiville's',*
The Kerryman, *21 October 2004)*


When we were growing up if you were caught talking to a boy you'd have to marry him: but times have changed, it has changed a lot.

My mother was married at fourteen years of age and it was a match. It was agreed around the fire and a match was made and she ended up marrying my father, he was always a good man to her. He was twenty-one when he got married. She had fifteen or sixteen children; she lost a couple of children.

*(Kerry Travellers' Development Project,* Do you no mydell? Poems, Stories & Pictures by Travellers in Kerry)

Marriage never shortened a man's life if he meets the right woman.

*(Éamon Kelly, 'Beyond the Horizon', in* Ireland's Master Storyteller: The Collected Stories of Éamon Kelly*)*


I have not had a bad life. A friend of mine was talking to a French woman in Ballydavid, and the French woman asked how long she had been married.

'Forty-four years,' said my friend.

'My God, what persecution,' said the French woman.

Well, it has been no persecution for me.

*(Bríd Bean Uí Cheallacháin in Brenda Ní Shúilleabháin's* Bibeanna: Memories from a Corner of Ireland*)*


This was a soul kiss …

What stunned me was the realisation that he had done this before. No one could kiss like that without practice.

My God, I thought, what if he isn't the incorruptible man I imagined but the horned Goat of Puck Fair?

But he was a goddam bishop, where had he learned all this?

*(Annie Murphy,* Forbidden Fruit*)*


You meet somebody, you fall in love with them, and you want to spend the rest of your life with them. It's no different to anybody else.

It should not be a big deal. I just hope that ten years after you announce your sexuality that nobody is still talking about it.

*(Martin Greenwood, who entered a civil partnership union with his partner James Bergin in 2012, interviewed by Aidan O'Connor. 'Being gay was never an issue',* Kerry's Eye, *29 January 2015)*

We will be married thirty years this August. I was sixteen years of age when I got married. We met in the village of Adare and a few months after that we got married and I had my first child at the age of seventeen. We were married in Croagh, County Limerick, an open-air wedding. It was a summer's day and we had got big tables and two big four-wheeled flat tops and all the barrels of drink were loaded on top of them. We had tables displayed with all the food and a six-tier cake. Over a hundred and fifty people attended and they came from all over. Everyone enjoyed themselves; the banjo and the melodeon played and everyone went home safely.

*(Kerry Travellers' Development Project,* Do you no mydell? *Poems, Stories & Pictures by Travellers in Kerry)*

How can I go aisy when my own grandchild is for sale like an animal?

*(Nanna in* Sive *by John B. Keane on the proposed arranged marriage for her granddaughter)*

There was a man who married one of five sisters. He did not know his wife, and as he was a bit nervous and excited in the church, he didn't remember her features very well. Later in the evening, with a few drinks taken, he was sitting at one side of the room, and the five sisters were on the other. He examined them for a while. He turned to the man beside him. 'Tell me,' he said, 'which one of them have I married?'

*('Marriage' from Anecdotes in Brenda Ní Shúilleabháin's* Bibeanna: Memories from a Corner of Ireland)

She moved in closer to me. Well, a sensation went through my body like I'd caught a live electric wire. When we were leaving the hall that night, I'd half a notion that the disease of love was lying in my bones, yes and in the two of us. Maybe I have enough said now.

I suppose the disease of love takes everyone by surprise. There was no weekend after that when the two of us weren't together.

*(Maidhc Dainín Ó Sé,* House Don't Fall on Me*)*

I'll put an end to the ball nights. I'll put an end to the porter balls and the Biddy Balls! While there are wheels under my trap I'll go into every corner of the parish … I'll bring 'em down out of the haysheds! It has come to my ears that young women of marriageable age in this parish have remarked 'How can we get men if we don't go to the balls?' I'll tell 'em how they can get men. I'll tell 'em how! They have only to come round to the sacristy to me any Sunday after Mass and I'll get plenty of men for 'em without any balls ...

*(Éamon Kelly quoting 'Fr Walsh', in* The Apprentice*)*

Your companion, you know, is a very, very special commodity especially when they're so precious and, like, for a good few years now before he died we were together day and night ... and I bought next door a rocking chair and at three and four o'clock in the morning he'd say, 'Mary, are you still there?' And I would be there.

*(Mary Keane [wife of John B.] in conversation with Gabriel Fitzmaurice, in Eugene O'Connell (ed.),* Cork Literary Review, *Volume XV, 2013)*

'Aiting the Gander' was a very enjoyable pre-nuptial function that went on to give the parties a chance of getting acquainted ...

If Béib was nice Juil took the cake, and I married her for love and in that way started the fashion in this locality.

But there were plenty of love matches that time too and plenty of love-making. How you'd know that is by the bluebells in the wood and the long grass on the slopes of the railway. They used to come in for a bit of flattening.

*(Éamon Kelly,* The Apprentice*)*

When people marry first and they're young, there is a certain conflict. And that conflict was very well-illustrated in the life of the Tailor and Ansty because the sexes are different and one complements the other. There is, when people get married first, a conflict and a flare-up but nature has provided for that, the coming together again and making it up is worth it.

But then as you get older and the family grow up and go away, then the relationship becomes much quieter, warmer, more understanding because you anticipate the other's desires. And there's the caring when one partner has to provide for the other in sickness.

*(Éamon Kelly,* The Kerryman, *19 November 1999)*

'I never,' said he, 'proposed marriage to any woman but one – my Mary.' I said to her, 'Are you engaged, Miss O'Connell?' She answered, 'I am not.' 'Then,' said I, 'will you engage yourself to me?' 'I will,' was her reply. And I said I would devote my life to make her happy. She deserved that I should – she gave me thirty-four years of the purest happiness that man ever enjoyed. My uncle was desirous I should obtain a much larger fortune, and I thought he would disinherit me. But I did not care for that. I was richly rewarded by subsequent happiness.

*(Daniel O'Connell's proposal to his penniless twenty-two-year-old cousin Mary O'Connell in 1800. William J. Daunt,* Personal Reflections of the Late Daniel O'Connell, MP*)*

I wish, darling, you were come home. I can't tell you how I feel without you. I am never so happy, darling, as I am with you for I doat [*sic*] of you, my heart's love, with the truest and fondest affection and no woman has such a husband as I have. It is impossible for any man to love a wife as you do yours, my dearest best of darlings …

> *(An extract from a letter to The Liberator Daniel O'Connell, while he was in Cork, from his wife, Mary, at Carhen, Kerry, 23 March 1804. Maurice R. O'Connell (ed.),* The Correspondence of Daniel O'Connell, Vol. 1, 1792–1814*)*

For my part the truth is that without you my heart is a complete void. I vegetate but I don't live.

> *(An extract from a letter from The Liberator Daniel O'Connell in Cork to his wife, Mary, at Carhen in Kerry, 20 August 1804. Maurice R. O'Connell (ed.),* The Correspondence of Daniel O'Connell, Vol. 1, 1792–1814*)*

I met my husband during a snowstorm, and there were plenty of those in Boston. I met him as he was shovelling snow off the sidewalk. I thought he would be a good worker anyhow! He was from Lispole …

> *(Eibhlín Bean Uí Bhrosnacháin in Brenda Ní Shúilleabháin's* Bibeanna: Memories from a Corner of Ireland*)*

If any two people can't get on and are badly met or matched, why in the name of God should they have to continue living together? It's very unfair to keep them hooked up like that. People are living their own lives in this country for the past ten years or so and that situation isn't going to change on the ground. Divorce doesn't make an iota of difference to many people. They don't care and they're living together anyway.

*(Jackie Healy-Rae in Donal Hickey's* The Mighty Healy-Rae*)*

We met on Sunday evenings and walked the quiet stretch by the river or picked whortleberries in Merry's Wood in October when juice stained our mouths a bluish purple. I loved her but I was never sure if she had a true wish for me.

*(Éamon Kelly,* The Apprentice*)*

And the worst of it all, Mr Marshall, is that she gives herself all the airs of a three hundred pound girl and she had but a hundred and fifty.

*(Callinafercy mother-in-law complaining to the landlord about her son's new wife in Samuel Hussey's* The Reminiscences of an Irish Land Agent*)*

I will go further, and seriously affirm my belief that the marriages in Kerry show a greater average of happiness than any which can be mentioned. To be sure there is the same dash after heiresses in Kerry that you see in Mayfair, and the young farmer who is really well-to-do is as much pursued as the heir to an earldom by matchmaking mothers in Belgravia. But the subsequent results are much more harmonious in Kerry.

*(Samuel Hussey,* The Reminiscences of an Irish Land Agent*)*


Cáit Sayers' boreen was like O'Connell Street with all the courting couples. You would need a ticket to get a space by the ditch.

*(Maidhc Dainín Ó Sé,* House Don't Fall on Me*)*


'Why does your brother not support you?'

'How could he support any one after bringing an empty woman to the house?'

*(An empty woman was one who came without a dowry on marriage. Samuel Hussey,* The Reminiscences of an Irish Land Agent*)*


I know what a man have to do who have no woman to lie with him. He have to drink hard, or he have to walk under the black sky when every eye is closed in sleep.

*(Thomasheen in* Sive *by John B. Keane)*

A fortnight after I met him he had a poem printed in *The Kerryman* called 'Two Eyes'. I remember saying to a friend of mine, I wonder whose eyes are they. Then I found out afterwards that the poem was about me ... On the second night of Listowel Races, when we'd both be flying busy behind the bar, we'd always take time to wish each other a happy anniversary.

*(Mary Keane,* The Kerryman, *12 February 1999)*


Experience has shown us here that the boy who displays too keen an interest in dancing or in mixed teenage parties is certain to make poor progress in his studies, to give poor value to his parents for the hard-earned money expended on his education and to be a bad influence on his fellow students.

In an effort to maintain a high standard of studies here, I intend to expel from the College immediately any boy who attends dances or mixed teenage parties, whether held during school terms or during holiday periods. Even if a boy has his parents' permission to attend such a dance or mixed teenage party, I will insist on his leaving here for good ...

*(An excerpt from a letter sent to parents or guardians of day pupils of Saint Brendan's College, Killarney, in 1966 by college president Right Rev. Monsignor John Moynihan, VG)*

Written after I was shot – Darling Nancy I was shot leading a rush up Moore Street, took refuge in a doorway. While I was there I heard the men pointing out where I was and I made a bolt for the lane I am in now. I got more than one bullet I think. Tons and tons of love dearie to you and to the boys and to Nell and Anna. It was a good fight anyhow.

Please deliver this to Nannie O'Rahilly, 40 Herbert Park, Dublin.

Good bye darling.

*(Note written by one of the key figures of the Easter Rising of 1916, Ballylongford-born Michael Joseph Rahilly, also known as The O'Rahilly, to his wife, Nancy, as he lay mortally wounded in a doorway in Sackville Lane near Moore Street in Dublin on the night of Friday 28/Saturday 29 April)*


He was like the falling star. The star fell at my feet.

*(Sheila McCarthy describes meeting her husband, Michael, in the Iveragh Ballroom, Cahersiveen, in the early 1940s, 'Still Valentines after 70 years',* Kerry's Eye, *12 February 2015)*


The first thing is no smoking or drinking and no arguments in the house.

*(Sheila's recipe for a long and happy marriage)*

The dowry was an important ingredient in a Sliabh Luachra-style marriage. Usually, the unmarried sister of the newly married husband of the incoming bride received it, and was in a position then to initiate match-making proceedings immediately, to find a home and a husband of her own ...

One dowry could generate up to five matches in one Shrove, and continue the good work at Easter or the next Shrove ...

After Shrove Tuesday came the 'Skellig Lists'. These were satires on those of marriageable age who had failed to marry before Shrove ...

*(Séan Ó Mathúna, 'Marriage Sliabh Luachra Style',*
Journal of Cumann Luachra*)*

*Con Houlihan on being asked if he had ever been in love:*
Every day of my life. I hate the word relationships or affairs. I have been in love in a big way several times. My heart is like a battle-field – what's left of it. I hadn't time to get married. I told you. I'm a hunter. My last girl-friend is now my friend-girl.

*(*The Kerryman, *19 June 1998)*

They first met in 1977, in The Oval on Abbey Street. Harriet was meeting a friend for coffee but, when she arrived, that friend – Maeve – had struck up a conversation with this vast, enigmatic figure at the bar.

'Con, this is my friend, Harriet.'

A giant hand reached towards her and, mischief in his smile, he asked, 'Are you bespoken?'

A devout Dublin football fan, she had become an avid reader of his column in the *Evening Press* since Heffo led the great, romantic city break-out three years earlier.

Con was taller than she had imagined. Before they parted, he'd invited her to a Jacques Berl supper in the Shelbourne Hotel.

Harriet's acceptance of his offer pushed open the door of a beautiful thirty-five-year story of companionship that would end only with his final breath in St James's Hospital last August.

*(Vincent Hogan, 'I can't tell you how much I miss him ... I'm like a lost soul', Con Houlihan's Ireland – The Lost Essays,* Irish Independent, *2 March 2013)*


The hard thing was to divorce my husband. He did not agree with anything I was doing. He was madly jealous about everything – the children, books and the cleaning woman ...

Divorce saves some people's lives. I was married fifteen years and I wasn't a day happy.

*(Lily van Oost, 'Lily of the Valley',* The Kerryman, *15 August 1986)*

You'd want an armoured car if you wore a pair of slacks. Do you know how long it is since he had a bath? A year! Imagine a whole year! He changes his shirt every Sunday and sleeps in it for the rest of the week.

*(Maimie describes her husband, in* The Field *by John B. Keane)*


She took me to Lourdes on the honeymoon. We lit a pile of candles and we went back twenty-five years later to quench them.

*(The late Dermot O'Callaghan of the Failte Hotel, Killarney, who married his wife, Eileen, on 10 October 1961,* The Kerryman, *15 February 1991)*


Katie married young to, as she said herself, a wild, brawny, mountain boy, with hair as black as a raven's wing, who could rise high into the air to gather a football, and a smile that would lure a linnet off a high tree. 'He died young, didn't he, Katie?' I said.

'He did, boybawn,' said Katie. Then she quoted a piece from an old Kerry poem:

*Would that I were young again to be a bride once more*
*To see again that smiling man calling to my door.*
*Truth shining in his eyes, oh happiness sublime.*
*But consumption took no pity on happiness like mine.*

Still, Katie and her brawny mountain man had ten children before the scourge of TB laid him low. There was no dole to draw, no pension, just the income from the little rocky mountain farm, and the sale of black turf in the nearby town.

*(Seán McCarthy, 'McCarthy's Women', The Kerryman, 6 July 1990)*

Marriage on the surface in many instances looks marvellous, but it isn't so marvellous at all because there's many an Irishman who can mingle the safe delights of matrimony with the perilous prurience of infidelity and, oddly enough, be ultimately honoured with a highly favourable mortuary card … But marriage, to survive, you must recognise it as a confrontation, an ongoing war between two people with short outbreaks of peace in between …

The biggest threat that I can see to marriage is outside issues. Marriage is a game for two. It doesn't need a referee. It doesn't need linesmen. When the ball is thrown in, let the two of them at it.

*(John B. Keane, The Late Late Show, 1989. Uploaded on YouTube by Listowel Arcade, 10 October 2011)*

My darling Love,

… I was detained in Court until past nine so that it was impossible for me to write. I do assure you I felt lonely at being any entire day without addressing myself to you and I have no other consolation than in thinking the more of the sweetest of her sex. Darling, if anybody were to read our Love letters they would perhaps laugh at us, but we have the happiness to know that instead of exaggerating any feeling the difficulty is to find expressions sufficiently strong to describe those affections which we really entertain for each other. At least, sweet love, it is literally so with me, for from my soul I do so doat of you ...

*(An extract from a letter from The Liberator Daniel O'Connell to his wife, Mary, at their Dublin home in Westland Row, 4 April 1809. Maurice R. O'Connell (ed.),* The Correspondence of Daniel O'Connell, Vol. 1, 1792–1814*)*

*The Bishop Eamonn Casey Affair:*

The story of Bishop Casey and Annie Murphy is a lurid and exceptional one, but basically it is about that question: if a man and a woman equally make a child, should they not equally bring that child through to adulthood? ...

I heard Peter Murphy on the radio and he sounded such a pleasant, intelligent young man. How terrible that he had no father. How terrible that nobody had the pleasure of being his father.

*(Nuala O'Faolain, 'Bishop Casey and the Conflict of Public and Private Lives', in Donovan, Jeffares and Kennelly (eds),* Ireland's Women: Writings Past and Present*)*

They put him in my arms and in that first instant I knew what millions of mothers before me had known: I would never give him up. I saw my darling child ... He was like Eamonn in every way.

*(Annie Murphy,* Forbidden Fruit*)*


'Look at him, Eamonn, he's beautiful. He's the most beautiful little baby. Hold him just for a minute.'

'No!' His horror sent a shiver through me. There was such a gulf between us. This child was everything to me and to him nothing ...

He could not see the child for the sin.

*(Annie Murphy,* Forbidden Fruit*)*


I acknowledge that Peter Murphy is my son and that I have grievously wronged Peter and his mother Annie Murphy.

I have sinned against God, His Church and the clergy and people of the dioceses of Galway and Kerry.

*(Statement issued by Bishop Casey on 11 May 1992)*


If your son is half as good a man as his father, he won't be doing too badly.

*(Gay Byrne,* The Late Late Show, *2 April 1993)*

I'm not too bad either, Mr Byrne.

*(Annie Murphy,* The Late Late Show, *2 April 1993)*

The Casey affair exposed clerical hypocrisy and double-dealing on a grand scale.

*(Gerard Colleran, 'Hard news',* The Kerryman 1904–2004
*anniversary publication)*

If he [Eamonn Casey] had one single weakness, that is the only one, that he might have a few extra drinks. If this intelligent lady came over from the States, it wouldn't be long before she'd have discovered this weakness. That's the way the man got trapped.

She took advantage of his drinking and there's no two ways about it. Eamonn Casey was a decent, honourable, fine man.

*(Jackie Healy-Rae interviewed by Liam Fay, 'The Kingdom's Kingmaker',* Hot Press, *31 May 1995)*

I'd love to see the man home. He did great work in London when I was there. I know because I met him once up in the building sites. There's a lot worse than Casey around, I'll tell you that much.

*(Dan Kennedy, Listowel, quoted in a vox pop in*
The Kerryman, *2 January 1998)*

## Sex, Marriage and other Shenanigans

*A selection from* The Little Book of John B. Keane:

An affair is like an air-filled toy balloon which takes off madly in all directions when its wind is released. It rasps, wheezes, snorts, squeaks and screeches with a passion unbridled and then flops on the floor, a parody of its former self.

An affair is a mere sneeze which gathers slowly and disperses quickly.

Given the option of attending a funeral or a sex orgy the dyed-in-the-wool Celt will always opt for the funeral.

The same God … gave man domination over the fowl and the brute, over every corner of the land and sea but man has no dominion at all over his own flute and the tunes it's likely to play and that's a thing all men must remember when shame reddens the cheek.

The double bed is the hatchery of every family plot, the blueprint for designing the features of offspring, the last refuge of the fractured marriage and a great place to hide under if you're a man on the run.

In its own time and in its own place and in conditions blessed by love the kiss will melt the icicles of frigidity and replace the pinched cheek with the amorous suffusion.

A play about sex in Ireland is always ahead of its time.

The secret of sex is not to take it seriously.

A married couple who don't look worn after a lifetime together have not been doing their job. They remind me of the footballer who comes off the field at the end of the game as fresh as when he first went on.

# AMONGST WOMEN

Women are like the ocean, peaceful and calm one minute and the next violent and raging.

*(John B. Keane,* The Little Book of John B. Keane*)*

The women of this area have always struck me as being strong, resolute and admirable. Even in the old days of the shawls, the women were powerful people, like our friend Méin. In modern times, with all due respect to men, the women are the leaders of this society. All voluntary activity in the area seems to be developed and spearheaded by women. It is not that men are not active, but you would be greatly aware of the women. They have taken their place in public life and that's a good thing.

*(Síle Bean Uí Mhaolchta in Brenda Ní Shúilleabháin's* Bibeanna: Memories from a Corner of Ireland*)*

I was throwing an eye at a couple of girls who were dancing near the stage. If you saw the wicked eye I got back from one of them. She'd kick the cart if a man went within twenty yards of her.

*(Maidhc Dainín Ó Sé,* House Don't Fall on Me*)*

These and everything else, the rag and taggle of the bone shop of the heart would be for the three women, the Three Graces who reared me.

But it wouldn't be enough. Art would fall short. Art would not have breath enough for the great glorious imaginative curses all three came up with when pressed – not the simple expletives of today, but threatening and eloquent phrases raging between heaven and earth, between hearth and ditch …

It was an extraordinary world, the world of my youth – as far-fetched now and as remote as Prospero's Island. And it was a world I have never met again anywhere, either in the bland 'Toil Dé' literature of Peig, the whispering drawing rooms of Jane Austen, or the intense novena-driven suburbs of Dublin or Cork.

We lived at a tangent, lateral to the main road, lateral perhaps in more ways than one.

There were no men in this world – men were either tradesmen or dead.

*(Anne Lucey, 'The Three Graces', Cúm)*

I never met my husband til the day I married him but it was a love-match til the day he died. And why shouldn't it, for he was a fine big man.

*(Peig Sayers,* An Old Woman's Reflections*)*

But to go back to 1908. One comical result of the news that a pension was coming in for everyone over seventy was that some women aged ten years in one night.

*(Éamon Kelly,* The Apprentice*)*


My mother used to go to other towns around begging and selling things from a basket. They used to buy the things to sell from a small shop in Castleisland like needles, thread, holy pictures, a bit of lace, hair combs, key rings and anything they thought they could sell. My mother and father's sisters, Nell and Meena, used to go to the fairs selling or telling fortunes. They had great times judging by the stories they used to tell us.

*(Kerry Travellers' Development Project,* Do you no mydell? Poems, Stories & Pictures by Travellers in Kerry*)*


I am ninety-two years of age and still working in my shop everyday! This old world premises, which includes a public house and grocery business in Castleisland, dates as far back as 1798. It is a three-hundred-year-old building, beautifully constructed in cut stone …

I never want to retire. The regulars keep me going, every day there's something. I give out to them and fight with them … but only sometimes! I enjoy it all.

*(Sheila Prendiville in Valeria O'Sullivan's* I am of Kerry*)*

Education could also change the position in which women were placed in relation to men. As women became more educated the reaction came: they asked: Why should we submit? The class of men who admire Paine and read Hume were not likely to give a very satisfactory reply. There was, there is, no merely natural reason why women should submit to men. Why should their will be law to any? By what right do they claim to rule? Let them be at least consistent in their infidelity ...

*(Sister Mary Francis Clare, born Margaret Anna Cusack and known as the Nun of Kenmare, in Irene ffrench Eagar's* The Nun of Kenmare*)*

When will something be done to remove the evil of unfairly paid work for women? How many cases of suicide, of literal starvation arose from the greed which would not pay fair wages to the poor workwoman? How many women were driven to a life they abhorred, simply to get bread?

*(Sister Mary Francis Clare in Irene ffrench Eagar's* The Nun of Kenmare*)*

A hardy breed of tramps (itinerants or travellers) frequented the localities of Kerry and Cork ... One morning in mid winter, I was going to assist at an early Mass and noticed one of their women folk washing a small baby in the icy water of a little stream beside the road. I told my mother when I came home.

She went to the place and brought the woman, her husband and another child to our house. She fed them and they stayed the night, sleeping on some straw on the kitchen floor. It was explained to me later that the woman had given birth to the baby during the night in a cart by the side of the road.

*(Jeremiah Murphy,* When Youth Was Mine: A Memoir of Kerry 1902–1925*)*


The Islanders tell the tale ... of the woman who had never stirred from her home, and on her first venture, coming to the crest of the pass and gazing over the spreading landscape, cried out: 'What a wide, weary place is Ireland!' and, frightened by the vastness of the revealed world, turned back for ever to her cosy, familiar Island.

*(Robin Flower,* The Western Island*)*


John B. Keane is the first Irish dramatist to treat Irish women in a context outside the big classical male fields, the heroic backgrounds of war, murder and revenge. At the very least he was the first not to overlook women in a society that institutionalised the overlooking of women.

*(Anne Lucey, 'Painting Irish Women's True Portrait',* The Kerryman, *12 February 1999)*

I have always been conscious of my freedom. My father gave us this appreciation of being free ... I always tell my children that the sky is the limit and I have told my daughters to go out and get professions, because I think it is very important for women to stand on their own two feet. Education is very important. That is where freedom is to be found, along with travel ...

Women have always been the underdogs and the scales can be balanced through education ...

*(Margaret Geaney in Jimmy Woulfe's* Voices of Kerry*)*


We Irish do not exactly cheer mothers minus wedding rings.

*(Doctor's remark to Annie Murphy,* Forbidden Fruit*)*


That is, I think, the greatest change in my life – the silence. All through the years, when I woke in the morning, the cows were lowing, the calves were noisy, the hens, the turkeys, the geese, everything was shouting to be fed in the morning. Now, I hear only the sound of the wind. It is strange, and it makes me feel sad.

*(Bríd Bean Uí Cheallacháin in Brenda Ní Shúilleabháin's* Bibeanna: Memories from a Corner of Ireland*)*


How could he let me, who had shared his bed, stay with our son in a place like this? A home for Unmarried Mothers! Where were the Unmarried Fathers? Surely not all the babies in this place were conceived by the Holy Ghost? Unmarried fathers must exist but they didn't have to have their noses rubbed in it. They were invisible like Eamonn. Not a line on his belly, a bead of milk on his breasts, a varicose vein on his leg, not a mark of paternity on him. Was this why men were such hypocrites?

*(Annie Murphy,* Forbidden Fruit*)*

My most important friendship is with my wife. We are friend and lover, which is a great relationship and she is the greatest woman ever to enter my ken. Without her I don't know what I'd be … All I know is that she has brought joy and colour into my life and we are extremely happy. We have had ups and downs, tragedies in our lives and all that, but we have survived. We will survive anything together.

*(John B. Keane in Jimmy Woulfe's* Voices of Kerry*)*

But we stayed together and we had love for each other through thick and thin and we would work away all through the day until we would be together at night and it was beautiful – the two of us, we might lie together or sit together or talk together. It was just working all day and waiting for that.

*(Mary Keane [wife of John B.] in conversation with Gabriel Fitzmaurice, in Eugene O'Connell (ed.),* Cork Literary Review, *Volume XV, 2013)*

As the President of Ireland, I respect her in a very special way. But I think this travelling all over the world is gone mad altogether ... I have nothing against the lady but she is gallivanting around the world too much. She's up in the air nearly as often as she is on the ground ... If she were Secretary General of the United Nations I'd expect her to be on the move. Maybe she has a post like that in the head. She's not up in the sky all that time for fun.

*(Jackie Healy-Rae commenting on President Mary Robinson in Liam Fay's 'The Kingdom's Kingmaker',* Hot Press, *31 May 1995)*

---

In the twilight of the November day that my grandmother died, the evening star hung like a bright lamp over the shoulder of Strickeen, the little mountain in whose shelter she had taken her first breath and, now, her last.

The star first came into view in the deepening blueness of the sky over the McGillycuddy Reeks as I drove the climbing road from Tralee towards her home at the Gap of Dunloe.

By the time I parked the car outside the house below Strickeen, the mountain was black and the celestial lantern shone all the clearer ...

When her coffin was carried out, the light spilled before her through the front door into the darkness of the night which hid Strickeen in its mantle.

The day she was buried was wet and windy and the ground was muddy underfoot in the old graveyard at the foot of the

McGillycuddy Reeks. I looked up from the grave at one stage and saw a ragged square of blue – as big as a good-sized field – open up in the cloudy sky.

*(Breda Joy, 'A woman who lived and died in the shelter of the mountains', The Kerryman, 1 January 1999)*


Nothing so affronts the female eye as that cataclysmic calamity of the culinary world, the sunken porter cake.

*(John B. Keane,* The Little Book of John B. Keane*)*


My hardest cross has been the loss of three of my children. It is hard to put your child down in the clay. But in my life, I have learnt that you have to accept the things that come your way. I have shed many tears, and tears heal. I am proud of my children, of how well they did at school, of how they all made a living. Although it is cruel to have to part with them, I have lovely memories.

*(Neil Bean Uí Uigín in Brenda Ní Shúilleabháin's* Bibeanna: Memories from a Corner of Ireland*)*


The unattached women of today burn up vodka and gin as if they had jet engines inside. If it made them drunk itself, but what happens is that they become more crafty.

*(John B. Keane,* The Little Book of John B. Keane*)*

My mother was a Quinn from near the Conor Pass. She was known as Katie. You notice nowadays that women tend to keep their maiden names on marrying, as part of the modern culture. But this was always the situation in the Gaeltacht. My mother was always known as Katie Quinn rather than Bean Uí Muircheartaigh. What is now considered modern, was part of the old Gaelic culture in Gaeltacht areas. It signified women's independence; they were persons in their own right.

*(Micheál Ó Muircheartaigh in Jimmy Woulfe's* Voices of Kerry*)*


They'll be in soon screeching for their Bacardis.

*(Elderly man overheard by author in Walsh's Bar, Knocknagoshel)*


I could see that she had her full share of the passion for children which is powerful in all women who are permanently and profoundly attractive.

*(J. M. Synge,* John M. Synge in West Kerry*)*


But my mother was the real power in the house and it was the same story with each of the neighbouring women; she took over and did the milking and the other jobs whenever Jimmy was in England and waited for money to come home. She was hugely and fantastically intelligent and none of us could ever match her … She would read for the neighbours all about the murder trials and with barristers' language and all thrown in she would be as good as Ann Doyle herself on television … There was once when she brought a laudatory discussion on the new priest to an abrupt end by claiming that she would have washed up after a *meitheal* in less time than it was taking him to wipe one chalice.

*(John Moriarty in Micheál Ó Muircheartaigh's* From Borroloola to Mangerton Mountain*)*


There are many Irish women like sports-cars with speeds of one hundred and fifty miles an hour but moving at only forty-five.

*(John B. Keane,* The Little Book of John B. Keane*)*


It was near the end of winter when I awakened. I was on my mother's back on the way to school for the first time. I was bundled up in a scarf and woollen cap, and my mother bore me along a cold winter road. The road was white and ice crackled beneath her feet.

*(Rory O'Connor,* Gander at the Gate*)*


The tinker's wife wouldn't be seen in the camp during the day, but she would come home about dinner time to cook a bite of food for her husband and the children. She would spend most of the day going from house to house with a big basket filled with saucepans, holy pictures, scapulars, blessed medals and shoelaces. Even though she would sell the goods in her basket, she wouldn't bring it home empty. Because if she sold a saucepan in a house she would ask for a grain of tea or sugar or a drop of milk to bring home to her little ones. Often she came to the school door and, to tell the truth, none of the teachers let her go away empty-handed.

*(Maidhc Dainín Ó Sé,* House Don't Fall on Me*)*

I sat at my window as they passed by after sentence of death had been pronounced; there was a large military guard taking them back to gaol, possibly forbidden to allow any communication with the three unfortunate youths. But their mother was there, and she, armed in the strength of her affection, broke through the guard. I saw her clap her eldest son, who was but twenty-two years of age; I saw her hang on the second, who was not twenty; I saw her faint when she clung to the neck of the youngest boy, who was but eighteen – and I ask what recompense could be made for such agony? They were executed – and they were innocent!

*(O'Connell's comments on the execution for murder of three Cremin brothers who he had unsuccessfully defended; William J. Daunt,* Personal Reflections of the Late Daniel O'Connell, MP*)*

The eldest of the family wouldn't have been more than sixteen. There were seven of us there. The youngest was born the March after he died, in November. She was an extraordinary woman because here she was, pregnant with her seventh child, her husband dead, she a widow in her forties, living on the side of the street in Cahirciveen, really facing very difficult times and she still did what she was asked. She was greatly admired and loved in the community here – I think much more than I ever could be. She had a way with people that I never really had. But they did love her and she them.

*(Former minister and TD John O'Donoghue describing his mother, Mary, whose husband Dan died on 10 November 1964 and whose county council seat she took.* Owen O'Shea's Heirs to the Kingdom*)*

I'm alone now but I'm free and not too many women can say that. But I need not be alone, and that's the beauty.

*(Maggie in John B. Keane's* Big Maggie*)*

John B. is married to a great human being, Mary. She is largely responsible for the fact that he is still living, writing, drinking, eating, talking, laughing, remembering, loving. She is an unfailing source of strength and support, a bright, witty, wise woman, with a heart full of tolerance, kindness and understanding.

*(Brendan Kennelly,* The Kerryman, *12 February 1999)*

I must have launched every fridge, cooker and car that was to be launched ... I was always business-minded. I was looking out for something to do but it wasn't easy because people never take models seriously. If you're sitting on a washing machine looking pretty one day and looking for a business opening the next, it isn't easy.

*(Jackie Lavin, 'Jackie returns to her Kerry roots',*
The Kerryman, *4 May 1990)*

His [Brendan Kennelly's] landmarks for his Ballylongford childhood are mostly female. There were the women living on either side of his house and his schoolteacher, Jane Agnes McKenna, who taught him languages. Such a love did she inculcate in her pupil that he hungrily read Latin, Greek, French and Irish. When he took Irish mythology for his PhD, he read the European myths too, Homer and Dante.

And then there was his mother. Her name was Bridie. She came from north Kerry and worked above in Cork as a nurse. At a dance in Ballybunion in 1931, she met a man from Scrolm Hill in the parish of Ballydonoghue who had returned from America. They wed and set up home in Ballylongford on the earnings of Timmy's Old Tin Shed, the garage where Mr Kennelly repaired cars and clocks.

One day, Bridie was standing in front of the range when the third of her eight children asked her: 'What is the secret of life?' She paused and thought before replying: 'Give as much love as you can.' He preserved that moment in a collection called *Begin*, the same poem that the monks of Glenstal Abbey recite every Christmas morning.

*(Justine McCarthy, 'The Keeper of the Flame',*
Irish Independent, *4 July 2001)*


In Kerry, the women, in 1917, participated in the anti-conscription campaigns. As the Anglo-Irish war flamed in violence Cumann na mBan grew and expanded in Kerry, outside of the large towns. By 1919/1920 there were branches all over north Kerry with young women flocking to the banner. Their work was vital for the campaign – the men were on the run, so the women provided the logistics of a military campaign. They were the eyes and ears of the IRA. They did all the intelligence work – dangerous work, as was the carrying of messages and dispatches from one company to another. Without these dispatch carriers the planning of the operations would have been next to impossible. They also carried arms, munitions, bombs and other armaments for Volunteer companies, to ambushes and planned operations. They were the 'minders' of arms dumps and the keepers of safe houses.

*(Dr Mary McAuliffe, describes the contribution of the women of Kerry to the fight for independence in* 'Cumann na mBan in Kerry', *a public lecture delivered in Listowel, 17 April 2014)*

No, no, Nora is not your ordinary tourist, visiting the old homestead, full of nostalgia for the years of long ago. Nora Brosnan McKenna has paid dues to this land of ours, and to the county of Kerry, where she bawled her first cry on the 17th of September 1905 …

Talking to Nora that March day in 1986, it was hard to realise the horrible punishment meted out to her as a young girl. She had survived incarceration, first in Mountjoy prison, later in Kilmainham jail. She has stood terrified, but determined, while Black and Tans raided her home three or four times every week, hiding her father in the stable with a horse who hated strangers. She had to watch the Tans as they doused her home with petrol, smashing, looting and rasing furniture, shivering out in the cold night until she found shelter with a neighbour.

*(Seán McCarthy's interview with Castlegregory woman, Nora Brosnan, on a visit to Kerry from her home in Milford, Connecticut,* The Kerryman, *2 March 1990)*


One evening, as I was leaving the chapel after benediction, I asked the Reverend Mother what a mother was. My question seemed to cause her some anxiety and she quickly brushed me along the corridor to supper.

*(Michael Clemenger,* Holy Terrors. A Boy. Two Brothers. A Stolen Childhood*)*

Although I hold a British passport I am in fact Irish, and the daughter of an Irish politician at that, which may account for a certain contrariness in my work. Many playwrights have become screenwriters; so I was a screenwriter and became a playwright.

*(Ronald Hayman quoting Bridget Boland in a chapter about the Kerry playwright, in K. A. Berney (ed.),* Contemporary British Dramatists*)*


John B. really gets under the skin of women. Himself and Shakespeare, they are the only two who have written for women. Living with Mary, that's how he understands.

*(Brenda Fricker,* The Kerryman, *12 February 1999)*

# HOME THOUGHTS FROM ABROAD

They left the mountain and the glen,
The Lassies and the fine young men.

*(John B. Keane,* Many Young Men of Twenty*)*

Out of sight, out of mind, in the context of Ireland's banished youth is a terrible indictment of the country's politicians … Well, the truth is that the politicians and the media have disgraced themselves in the neglect of the real Irish problem of emigration. Apart from the shameful £5 travel tax which all emigrants have to pay, there is the situation where the everyday task of ensuring that the day to day needs of the forced emigrants are taken care of is totally neglected.

*(John Barrett, 'London Calling',* The Kerryman, *5 January 1990)*

Everybody dreads getting that phone call of something wrong at home and not being able to travel back.

*(An undocumented Kerrywoman in New York, who hadn't been home in eleven years and had not seen her father in that time,* Kerry's Eye, *27 November 2014)*

It's a start but it's very disappointing for those who don't qualify. Nobody is going to risk going home. Being undocumented here is just a catalyst for other problems. Unless you've walked in these people's shoes, it's hard to understand. Some people haven't seen their parents for 20 years. They're just hoping they can hang on for another year.

*(Orla Kelleher from Kilgarvan, who runs the Aisling Irish Community Centre in Yonkers, New York, reacts to the announcement of new immigration rules in the USA,* Kerry's Eye, *27 November 2014)*

For many another in South Kerry and, indeed, elsewhere, a single ticket to Kingsbridge station, and a berth on the Holyhead boat had become a way of life. I was just one of the tens of thousands who were forced to emigrate during those bleak years of economic depression that followed World War II.

*(John Curran,* Just My Luck*)*

After the war in 1948, America opened up for emigration, and all the young people left. A place is never desolate until the youth leaves. Very few of them came back to stay.

*(Bríd Bean Uí Cheallacháin in Brenda Ní Shúilleabháin's* Bibeanna: Memories from a Corner of Ireland*)*

I looked west at the edge of the sky where America should be lying, and I slipped back on the paths of thought. It seemed to me now that the New Island was before me with its fine streets and great high houses, some of them so tall that they scratched the sky; gold and silver out on the ditches and nothing to do but gather it. I see the boys and girls who were once my companions, walking the street and laughing brightly and well contented …

*(Maurice O'Sullivan,* Twenty Years A-Growing*)*


I knew it was the last day: I was about to depart for a different world. It was also the last day that I worked with my father.

At about six o'clock we raked the embers of the fire together and quenched them with what water we had left over, and with what tea remained in the kettle. I was pierced with an infinite sadness.

*(Con Houlihan, 'Fond farewells – parting is such deep sorrow',
in* Windfalls*)*


Killarney emigrant Kathleen Cherrett returned to her native town this week after an absence of almost fifty years to pay a final visit to her parents' grave at Muckross Abbey.

Kathleen (née Hartnett) was saddened to find the town had changed beyond recognition but was pleased to fulfil her wish to make the nostalgic pilgrimage.

'It's not Killarney in my eyes anymore, it's not,' she said wistfully. 'I wish they had left it the way it was so I could go into a shop and say, 'Do you remember me?'

Kathleen was just fourteen years old when she left Killarney to go and live in Somerset with her eldest sister, Nora Hartnett. She returned home sixteen years later for her mother's funeral but had not been back again until this week.

*(Kerry's Eye, 9 September 2004)*


I managed fine. I can speak English when it suits me.

*(Con Houlihan on being asked if taking up a teaching post in a preparatory school in Hastings represented a culture shock,*
The Kerryman, *19 June 1998)*


I came to Broadway at 92nd Street and I stayed there with my aunt and sisters in St Gregory the Great Parish. I didn't like New York at first. I couldn't get over the subway, how old-fashioned it was in comparison to the London Underground. The seats were made of straw and it would stick up your backside; and we were all packed in like cattle and people were much rougher back then, although they were more refined than they are now, I suppose …

The Kerryman's Association ran a charter and it was the first of its kind from New York to Dublin. I was lucky to get leave off the job because my foreman, who was from Westmeath, hadn't been to Ireland since 1927 and of course they had to let him go. Luckily they let me go too. He hadn't seen his mother in over thirty years and the only way he would know her was that she was to tie a white handkerchief around her wrist. I'll always remember walking across the tarmac in Dublin Airport that day and seeing this little old lady all dressed in black waving the white hankie at a son she would hardly recognise. That's the price of immigration [*sic*].

*('Mike (Bobby) Cremin', extract from an interview in New York on 29 January 2006, in Finbarr Bracken's* Ballinskelligs Remembered*)*

My mother was the most important influence on my youth, I think. She was a beautiful red-headed woman who had emigrated to America, with her older sister, when she was fifteen.

She settled really well, and the first thing she bought was a melodeon. Along with Seán a' Chlasaigh, a neighbour from Ventry, she used to play for silent movies in the cinemas in New York, as well as working during the day. She was glamorous and well dressed, and loved America.

*(Peig a' Rí, Bean Mhic Ginneá, in Brenda Ní Shúilleabháin's* Bibeanna: Memories from a Corner of Ireland*)*

And the danger was there. Not so much at the fighting at Bull Run as down the mines in Bute, Montana. Patey Murrell told me that he heard his uncle saying that the horses pulling the trolleys down the mines in Bute worked a far shorter day than the men, and the quality of the food they got was better. You see if a horse died of overwork or starvation the Company would have to buy another one, but if a man died there was plenty more waiting outside the gate.

*(Éamon Kelly,* In My Father's Time*)*

Travel agents were called shipping agents in those days. There was a shipping agent at every crossroads. It was basically all emigration business – nothing else. There was no such thing as a return ticket in this period [1890s and early 1900s]. Every ticket was a single ticket …

The guy who emigrated was a twopence a day man. These men had very little money and were paid about a twopence a day. Our tickets show it was labourers and housemaids who emigrated. No fellow with money emigrated.

Public transport was unheard of when those early emigrants paid for their passage in Cornelius Counihan's pub and had their last drink with neighbours and friends on this side of the Atlantic. They rode to Cobh on donkeys and ponies and were greeted by opportunists who knew the animals were up for grabs on the quaysides because they wouldn't be travelling to the New World.

*(Travel agent Vincent Counihan,* The Kerryman, *22 January 1988)*

While Mick O'Connell has a fierce love of his island home, he has left the sheltering harbour to work abroad on two occasions.

After the cable station closed, he worked on the winter sugar beet campaign in Peterborough, Northamptonshire, in 1966/67. His memory from that time is of the open way the Englishmen spoke to him of their private lives – petty things like how much money they were giving up at home.

He found their openness very alien to what he was used to at home, and very amusing.

After he returned home, he made his living from farming and fishing until the early 1980s when he went to work in construction in the US. His contact at the time was Tommy Hennessy of Ballylongford.

His three children were born before he left and, during the two years he was away, he returned home for holidays and special family occasions. He describes the decision to go abroad as 'semi-voluntary' as he could have made ends meet without going.

'Many men who did leave home worked away in England to keep the home fires burning,' he said. 'They were only home for the holidays. I met a young fellow once and he said he never knew his father. That was sad.'

He speaks warmly of the late John Kerry O'Donnell from Camp who, he said, fostered more than anyone else links between Gaelic football people in New York and in Kerry and all parts of Ireland.

Mick worked on multi-storey buildings – up to fifty storeys above the noisy New York streets – and found the mix of nationalities very interesting.

*('Home thoughts and life abroad',*
The Kerryman, *18 February 2000)*


Lonesome was no name for it … He'd be surrounded on the platform by his friends, and when the time came for him to board the train he'd start saying goodbye to those on the outside of the circle, to his far out relations and neighbours, plenty of gab for everyone, but as he came in in the circle, to his cousins, to his aunts and his uncles, the wit and the words would be deserting him. Then he'd come to his own family, and in only what was a whispering of names, he'd say goodbye to his brothers and sisters. Then he'd say goodbye to his father, and last of all to his mother. She'd throw her two arms around him, a thing she hadn't done since he was a small child going to school, and she'd give vent to a cry, and this cry would be taken up by all the women along the platform. Oh, it was a terrifying thing for a small child like me to hear.

*(Éamon Kelly,* In My Father's Time*)*


At several stations girls and boys thronged in to get places for Queenstown, leaving parties of old men and women wailing with anguish on the platform. At one place an old woman was seized with such a passion of regret, when she saw her daughters moving away from her for ever, that she made a wild rush after the train; and when I looked out for a moment I could see her writhing and struggling on the platform, with her hair over her face, and two men holding her by the arms.

Two young men had got into our compartment for a few stations only, and they looked on with the greatest satisfaction.

'Ah,' said one of them, 'we do have great sport every Friday and Saturday, seeing the old women howling in the stations.'

*(J. M. Synge,* John M. Synge in West Kerry*)*

They were poor sailors and try as they might they couldn't keep the food down. Their time was spent at the ship's rail retching emptily into the sea. The half-circle of white foam at the base of Sceilig Mhichíl was their last glimpse of Ireland. They promised to write when they had settled in America and when they got work they would send some money.

*(Éamon Kelly,* The Apprentice*)*

A lot of young people going away at that time looked upon America as a place or state of punishment where some people suffered for a time before they came home and bought a pub, or a farm or married into land or business.

*(Éamon Kelly, 'Shrovetime',* Ireland's Master Storyteller: The Collected Stories of Éamon Kelly*)*

When I caught the cattle boat from Dun Laoghaire to England sixty-eight years ago, there was no talk about the diaspora in relation to the exodus of thousands of people from the shores of Ireland onto the work floors of Britain looking for work – reminiscent of the days of the dark satanic mills. When we arrived at Euston there was no Pope's Brass Band to meet us, no welcome, advice, help or financial assistance for us. We were thrown to the wolves. When we went looking for work we usually got jobs with the lowest pay, the longest hours and the poorest working conditions. In those days 'No Irish wanted' notices were common, as were bug-ridden mattresses. When it came to the welfare of the Irish emigrants during this period, the Irish government had a very poor record. No wonder the lark sang sad songs.

The millions of pounds that the Irish emigrants sent back to Ireland over the decades not only put food on the table and kept a roof over the heads of needy and destitute families but also kept the Irish economy afloat and boosted their invisible earnings. Let's not forget our compatriots; those who slept rough on the streets, who lie in unmarked graves and who suffered long, lingering and painful deaths as a consequence of unknowingly working with carcinogenic agents.

I ask the newly appointed Diaspora Minister, Jimmy Deenihan, to request the Executive Council of Dáil Éireann to proclaim a National Holiday or erect a memorial in honour of the sacrifices we emigrants made. It's long overdue – do it now.

*(Killarney emigrant Tony Horgan, 31 July 2014,*
*a letter sent to the Kerry media)*

In the front carrier of his bicycle he had a big parcel for us from our aunts in Dittmar's Boulevard, Astoria, New York. It had small items of wearing apparel, a tie for my father, a colourful apron for my mother, a cotton dress for my sister and knee breeches and jacket with a belt at the back for my brother and me. There was a doll and a small metal brightly painted carriage drawn by two horses with little wheels on their hooves so that we could run the carriage on the table or on the floor. There was a letter, too, with a robin redbreast Christmas card, and when the card was opened out popped three ten dollar bills, which was a small fortune to us. The letter made enquiries about our health and it was signed Mary, Margaret and Elizabeth.

*(Éamon Kelly,* The Apprentice*)*

The emigrant has been the theme of song and story. He has also been one of the finest recruits of the United States, whilst he is a stigma on English politics, and a drain on the land which in all Europe can least afford to spare him.

*(Samuel Hussey,* The Reminiscences of an Irish Land Agent*)*

My father's brother, Uncle Dan, spent most of his life in New York but he was just the same and rarely sent home a letter that didn't include a picture of a favourite horse. For a long number of years Dan and his brother, Michael, operated a bar on 53rd

Street and Third Avenue and that was when daily opening was allowed for twenty hours or more. The usual arrangement was for Dan to take charge at night to allow him time in the mornings for tending to his horse and riding in the park; he always kept a horse ... His horse *Fancy Boy* was always on Fifth Avenue for the St Patrick's Day parade.

*(Micheál Ó Muircheartaigh,* From Borroloola to Mangerton Mountain*)*

When you consider the scale and depth of the Irish overseas, and our long history of repeated ebbing and flowing from our borders, we can all agree that having a comprehensive government policy in place is timely and welcome.

*(Minister for the Diaspora Jimmy Deenihan addresses the Seanad on 'Global Irish: Ireland's Diaspora Policy', 10 March 2015)*

I sat in a corner; across from me in a far corner was a man who obviously had spent the day battling with the obdurate clay of London – his brown boots were liberally daubed with yellow clay.

He had red hair and the sideburns that were the logo of the Irish navvy; his face was the product of sun and wind; he could have been any age between thirty-five and fifty.

He took out his cigarettes and matches and gave himself up to the anodyne of ale and tobacco.

For the fleetingest of moments our eyes met – and again I suspected that telepathy is a relic of the age before man invented language.

He said – and I said – without speaking: 'We know each other.'

*(Con Houlihan, 'Golden days and nights in the Street of Romance', in* Windfalls*)*

Lying on my bed after a long day's work, I thought of the thousands of people who left the coast of Ireland to make their living in foreign countries. People who grew up with the freedom of the glens and the mountains. The song of the birds and the breaking of the waves against the cliffs behind them. With no sights to see in cities like London but big brick buildings. A black colour on them from the smut of industry. The noise of the machines and the bustle of the people; and yet, loneliness in the middle of the crowd. I was thinking of my father and my mother and they sitting beside the fire, the pipe in my father's mouth and smoke billowing from it.

*(Maidhc Dainín Ó Sé,* House Don't Fall on Me*)*

Take your shovel with you or you'll be without it. Your eye would be picked out of your head if your back was turned …

I put my shovel on my shoulder exactly as if I were earthing the spuds at home and walked across the site …

There was a man up there before him he thought was too slow. He let a fearsome shout out of him: 'Can you work any faster, you lazy bastard? Your mother should have drowned you when you were a baby.'

'Look at that poor unfortunate,' said Colm, 'and the abuse he got from that blackguard. This is his first day on the job. Oh wisha, that fellow will come to a bad end and I hope to God I'll be around to see it.'

*(Maidhc Dainín Ó Sé's account of a construction site in Camden Town*, House Don't Fall on Me*)*


The official slap-on-the-back for the government on delivering to the people of Killarney a brand new fire station took place last Friday.

When it comes down to it, official openings by the state are but a product of the propaganda machine. Yet another strand of the infinitely varied and painfully transparent political charade …

Blandness is the key note. For God's sake, don't mention cutbacks …

Consider the message delivered to Environment Minister Pádraig Flynn last Friday by county council chairman, Éamon Barry: 'If there is a message we would like to give the minister, it's that Killarney and the surrounding district are more beautiful in the winter than the summer,' said Colr Barry.

Granted Colr Barry was operating in line with the shallow

expectations of speeches on such occasions. Granted the snow-covered mountains looked exceptionally beautiful.

The mountains were beautiful these last few weeks but they are a shade too distant from Kilburn High Road, Willesden Green and Cricklewood where the majority of the town's young voters are earning a living.

Torc Waterfall was magnificent in full flood after the rains but a lot of water will have flowed on down into the Middle Lake before the illegal Killarney aliens in the Bronx and Boston will run the risk of returning home.

And Pádraig Flynn has looked over the fine new fire station and returned to Dublin happy in the knowledge that Killarney is more beautiful in the winter than in the summer.

*(Breda Joy, 'And for God's sake don't mention cutbacks',*
*The Kerryman, 19 February 1988)*

The front door of our terraced house in Cricklewood was like a gateway between two very different worlds. Outside on the doorstep you stood five miles north of Buckingham Palace in a busy, noisy London suburb, and, in those days, the 1950s, it was still foggy London Town. But when you opened the door and entered the house, you could just as easily have been three miles west of Annascaul. Steam from the bacon and cabbage simmering on the stove settled as a mist on the kitchen windows and obscured the world outside …

You see with names like Sullivan, O'Connor and O'Shea,

we'd be considered 'Irish' by our English neighbours but, with our English accents, back in the land of our forefathers we're 'The Returned Brit' or a 'Plastic Paddy'. Nobody, it seems, wants to claim us, so where is 'home' and who the heck are we?

I'm proud of my Irish background and I feel connected to Ireland in a real way. I grew up listening to stories and songs from Ireland every bit as much as my cousins in Kerry. I'm sure my Irish background informs my way of seeing and relating to the world. I feel at home under the changing Irish skies and I miss them when I'm away.

But are these the things that make us feel comfortable in our own skin? I'm not so sure and I don't mind if you call me a 'Plastic Paddy'. It won't keep me awake at night.

*(J. J. O'Shea, 'Plastic Paddy', a documentary broadcast on* Radio Kerry, *17 March 2014)*


The Cricklewoods are coming.

*(Auntie Kitty (O'Shea), Castlegregory, signalling the arrival of the London O'Sheas on their summer holidays. J. J. O'Shea, 'Plastic Paddy')*


I arrived in London on the morning after the Birmingham bombs … The tabloids were full of 'the bloody Irish'.

That was on a Thursday morning and I played rugby on the Saturday for London-Irish out in a place called Camberley – a nice settled respectable place. We got terrible abuse. People were inside drinking beer and watching the television which was showing Ireland playing New Zealand in Lansdowne Road. Every so often they would come out and start shouting at the Irish. It was understandable, I think, in the context of the Birmingham bombs.

*(Dick Spring in Stephen Collins'* Spring and the Labour Story*)*

The announcement last month of €12.5 million in next year's budget to support emigrants and engage with the diaspora worldwide is a significant achievement. It means we can maintain the level of Emigrant Support Programme funding and we have secured an additional €1 million for new diaspora projects and initiatives.

Of course, support would not be possible without the ongoing, dedicated work of the Irish centres and other organisations here in New York and throughout the US. On behalf of the Irish Government, I thank you for your important work in supporting our community here. Thank you also for your part in promoting Irish culture and preserving our heritage in the US.

*(Minister for the Diaspora Jimmy Deenihan announcing that Irish emigrants in the US are to receive support of over €1.8 million. Press release issued by Department of the Taoiseach and Foreign Affairs, 6 November 2014)*

I am a naturalized American, like so many millions of others from Ireland, Italy, Russia and elsewhere. I came with great hopes to this land of freedom and equality. All of us are still fighting to make those hopes come true. America had the know-how to produce the weapons of victory; we have the know-how to rid this country of the dregs of religious and racial hatred. The early Irish immigrants were discriminated against; the Negro people are still being kicked around and denied their rights. Such things have no place in America. We must never let up our fight to get rid of these manifestations of Nazism. It is everybody's fight.

*(Address of trade unionist Mike Quill to a community-based conference in the USA in 1945. Shirley Quill,* Michael Quill, Himself: A Memoir*)*

# WORDS OF WISDOM

As the old saying goes, 'Bitter the tears that fall but more bitter the tears that fall not'.

*(Maurice O'Sullivan,* Twenty Years A-Growing*)*

There is no cowardice worse than the cowardice of parents who will not face up to the facts, who refuse to recognise that rearing children to be useful members of society is a full-time, complicated, sensitive vocation without parallel in the whole range of serious callings.

*(John B. Keane,* The Little Book of John B. Keane*)*

There's no bone in the tongue but it often broke a man's nose.

*(Éamon Kelly,* source unknown*)*

And by the way a woman's tongue is something that doesn't rust.

*(Peig Sayers,* An Old Woman's Reflections*)*

There is so much good in the worst of us and so much bad in the best of us that it evens out.

*(A piece of wisdom quoted by my neighbour, Tom Herlihy)*


If a man has a spade in his hand and an interest in his work, he will not have a gun or a revolver.

*(Sister Mary Francis Clare in Catherine Ferguson's* Margaret Anna Cusack (The Nun of Kenmare): Knock, November 1881–December 1883*)*


I don't think you can achieve anything in this world without being intensely dedicated. And even then you can't be sure, as what is called 'failure' is always waiting. But I don't have much respect for either failure, or for what is called success. But I do respect somebody who realises himself or herself and brings to fruition whatever promise God gave them.

*(Brendan Kennelly in Jimmy Woulfe's* Voices of Kerry*)*


There is no doubt but youth is a fine thing though my own is not over and wisdom comes with age.

*(Maurice O'Sullivan,* Twenty Years A-Growing*)*

Bhí sé uasal, íseal. He was noble and humble.

*(A Blasket Island accolade)*


To become a really whole person we must be still and face the fear and hurt inside us. Having a place which allows us to do this, to quietly sit and listen to our own depths …

Time allows the light to dawn out of the darkness, only with the help and support of people can we learn to be safe and come to realise the shadows only exist because there is light.

*(Clo O'Keeffe-Lyons in Valerie O'Sullivan's* I am of Kerry*)*


I'll always remember myself the day long ago when I came face to face with Looney Mick, an old recluse, who lived in a hut behind Deernagh Lake. He had a beard that reached to his knees, and strange eyes. Only six years old at the time, I panicked and started to run, gashing my right knee on a sharp rock. I ran, fast as the wind, to Katie's kitchen, where she packed the cut with spider's web, and tied a cloth around it. I started to give out about Looney Mick, but Katie soon stopped me. 'Mick is no looney,' she said. 'He just hears a different voice to you or I.' Then she said something I have never forgotten. 'Always remember, young Seán, every crow has a different caw, and every caw finds a different crow.'

*(Seán McCarthy, 'McCarthy's Women',*
The Kerryman, *6 July 1990)*

If you weigh the character of the detractor against that of his victim you'll find that the latter always comes out on top.

*(John B. Keane,* The Little Book of John B. Keane*)*

All you have is your word. If you haven't a word, you have nothing.

*(Jackie Healy-Rae, as quoted by his son, Danny, at his funeral in Kilgarvan on 8 December 2014, and recorded by the author)*

I never promise anything without having the intention of keeping my promise. I think it's ugly if you don't … I am happy with almost nothing. If I have inspiration I am the happiest woman in the world.

*(Lily van Oost/Lily of the Valley,* The Kerryman, *15 August 1986)*

It is a religion for poets and drunks and people who sense the inadequacies of reason and logic.

*(Catholicism according to Brendan Kennelly, 'The Keeper of the Flame',* Irish Independent, *4 July 2001)*

Sky is plentiful but we must see it.

*(Seamus de Faoite, 'Sky is Plentiful', in* The More We Are Together*)*

My mother crossing the yard, holding turf and eggs, fire and life, in her upturned, cross-over apron, and cows coming up the road, my father's eleven cows, and my father walking behind them, walking slowly, because cows in calf, old short-horn cows that are heavy in calf, that's how they walk, to watch them walking you'd think 'twas the Dingle mountains they were carrying inside them.

That's how my father learned womb-waiting. That's where the dangerous wildness that used to be in him left him. Sitting on a three-legged stool against the stall wall behind his cows sitting there at night, listening to them chewing the hay or chewing the cud, that's where my father came to dh'end a thinkin'. That's where his wisdom came to him.

*(John Moriarty,* Turtle was Gone a Long Time*)*

'Problems like yours, Annie,' he said, 'don't go away. Unless you talk them out, they'll follow you all your life. One day, when you're least expecting it, they pop up and' – he gestured eloquently to his own throat – 'strangle you.'

*(Bishop Eamonn Casey in Annie Murphy's* Forbidden Fruit*)*

Kids are quick enough to hop-step into stride with life away from the full stop of a grave.

*(Seamus de Faoite, 'Sky is Plentiful',*
*in* The More We Are Together*)*

We accepted that [being childless] as the will of God, but I think it affected me more than my husband. I suppose the only thing I can say is that if I didn't have them to make me laugh, I didn't have them to make me cry.

*(Bríd Bean Uí Mhuircheartaigh in Brenda Ní Shúilleabháin's* Bibeanna: Memories from a Corner of Ireland*)*

Now even I, who have always loved a challenge and had nothing to lose, paled at the prospect and then I opened a card which had been left on my desk. It was a picture of a huge dragon with a tiny little armoured knight with a sword drawn looking up at the beast and challenging him. The caption was 'no guts – no glory'.

*(Maureen Erde,* Help! I'm an Irish Innkeeper*)*

I believe all addictions come under the one heading, as people take substances to kill the pain of living … If you were to ask me, I would never say anybody is an alcoholic. I do not like the idea of labelling anybody.

*(Sister Consilio in Jimmy Woulfe's* Voices of Kerry*)*

My mother used to tell me if you had any success to 'walk easy when your jug is full'.

*(Bryan MacMahon in Gabriel Fitzmaurice's* Voices of Kerry*)*

I strongly believe that if we were given the choice, we would not grant permission to contaminate our fruit and vegetables, mistreat our meat, pollute our homes and water supply. Each little step we take in our homes and communities has a ripple effect on our global community.

*(Mary O'Riordan in Valerie O'Sullivan's* I am of Kerry*)*


I love football. I love drinking and rogues and fellas that will not answer you. Abuse, curses, insults, blessings, all these things that have the mark of intensity.

*(Brendan Kennelly, 'The Keeper of the Flame',*
Irish Independent, *4 July 2001)*


As a young child my father often told me: Tóg go bog é agus bogfaidh sé chugat. The essence of my father's message was that if we say 'Yes' to life and not resist or fight it, then life will come freely, gently and fully.

My strongest memory of Kerry is of people who had a great sense of place and a sense of presence of living life fully. I was taught more by deed than word, that there is a time for everything and if we live fully in the now we will live freely, responsibly and with integrity. What happens here, now, is my responsibility. It is not a matter of doing great things: it is a matter of doing or saying small things with responsibility and courage.

*(Sr Stanislaus Kennedy in Valerie O'Sullivan's* I am of Kerry*)*

My wife, Margaret, and my brother, Joe, arrived at the hospital around midnight. At that stage, I seemed to know exactly what my problem was because I remarked lightheartedly: 'I am all right. I've only broken my neck.' I honestly believed that breaking one's neck was no different from breaking an arm or a leg …

The struggle was never going to be easy or pleasant but I resolved to make the best of whatever time was left. I could so easily have been killed outright in the accident but by a miracle of fate I was still alive. Somehow I never reached the point where I wanted to die. Life was still sweet even if it was going to be a bitter kind of sweetness …

Life and health are precious gifts and should never be abused because once irreparably damaged they can never be restored. Prior to my accident I was like many more people worrying about trivialities. But now I am looking at life through different eyes and I can see the world filled with many beautiful things I never knew existed.

*(John Curran,* Just My Luck*)*


You can't teach an old dog new tricks but when his mentors are the mounting years he will learn to share the hearth with the cat.

*(John B. Keane,* The Little Book of John B. Keane*)*

I find that with most people growing older and I find it myself, there is a preoccupation with one's end because, as you go down the road, you know it cannot be very far away. There's a preoccupation with that. You think about it every day. When I was a youngster, my mother loved the Friary in Killarney and she used to tell us – I don't know if it's true or not – that the Friars used to come out and dig a sod of their grave every day.

*(Éamon Kelly,* The Kerryman, *19 November 1999)*

Suddenly I remembered an incident that had happened when I was a small child in Ireland. I was in town in Tralee and I found a threepenny bit on the pavement outside a shop. I was going to go in and give it to the shopkeeper when my grandmother said, 'It's for yerself – sure if God hadn't intended it for you, do you think he'd have left you find it?'

*(Maureen Erde,* Help! I'm an Irish Innkeeper*)*

There are people who have died long before they sigh themselves away on a last breath: the old man – my father – lived all the time. With his last breath he gave the word 'Right' up to my mother's hovering face. 'Right' was his word for acceptance or for challenge.

*(Seamus de Faoite, 'Sky is Plentiful',*
*in* The More We Are Together*)*

I have no real plan for my life, none, and I am so calm in myself. I take every day as it comes. I thank God for the company, and for the chat, and I will keep my door open as long as I can.

> *(Máirín na Yanks Ní Mhurchú in Brenda Ní Shúilleabháin's* Bibeanna: Memories from a Corner of Ireland*)*

When the fact that he [Éamon Kelly] is a vegetarian is raised, he lists famous vegetarians including Plato, George Bernard Shaw, Tolstoy, Buddha and, finally with a smile, Hitler. He was influenced by friends of his in the theatre who were vegetarians. Loving nature so much, it went against the grain to eat them or to cause them pain.

> *(Breda Joy,* The Kerryman, *19 November 1999)*

Our new home looked on to the river, the Feale, at the back. I wonder if having been born there and living within sight and sound of a river gave me my great love of water? I have never in later life, felt lonely anywhere if water was my companion on a walk, or could be seen in a landscape.

> *(Bertha Beatty,* Kerry Memories*)*

Please mix me a stomach potion that will stop history repeating itself.

> *(John B. Keane,* The Little Book of John B. Keane*)*

It has been suggested to me by a lady who knows Kerry well that the consumption of drink might be diminished if a law were passed forcing the publicans to sell food.

*(Samuel Hussey,* The Reminiscences of an Irish Land Agent*)*


A person is a unique creation made by God. I believe that. And I think when you confront a person, whether it be a student, a man in a jail or a person in a pub, you are confronting a mystery who is unknown to you, a complete stranger. You can label him and say he is an eejit, a drunk, or a bore and walk out of his presence. But that is not enough for me – I genuinely try to appreciate the strangeness of others. That is why I keep on writing poetry. Because to me poetry is about appreciating strangeness. And I got this in many respects out of alcoholism. I got it out of being in a mental hospital. I got it out of knowing that out there in society there are a lot of people suffering from all kinds of things which they can't afford to reveal to their children or to themselves. The word I use is strange, and strangeness is stimulating to me. I would never take anybody for granted.

*(Brendan Kennelly in Jimmy Woulfe's* Voices of Kerry*)*


When the goat gets into the temple, he doesn't stop until he goes on the altar.

*(Maidhc Dainín Ó Sé,* House Don't Fall on Me*)*

Do you know that anybody who interferes with the travelling people has no luck for it? They are the Irish that Cromwell evicted out of their homes and land.

*(Maidhc Dainín Ó Sé quoting his primary school teacher, in* House Don't Fall on Me*)*


No! No! No! I will never let men do the business of horses if I can help it! Don't touch that harness, you vagabonds! I am trying to elevate your position, and I will not permit you to degrade yourselves.

*(Daniel O'Connell remonstrates with supporters who wanted to draw his carriage on Cork's Great Western Road in September 1840. William J. Daunt,* Personal Reflections of the Late Daniel O'Connell, MP*)*


… he had never allowed himself the luxury of inhabiting an ivory tower with books walling him away from 'real life'. He credits his breakdown at 22 with keeping him grounded ever after.

'Getting sick helped me,' he says. 'If I didn't get that breakdown, I'd be a bookworm. It gave me a great understanding of all kinds of illness.'

*(Monsignor Pádraig Ó Fiannachta,* The Kerryman, *12 June 1998)*

I was ordained into the Church of God, not into the Church of Ireland. To me, all people matter, particularly the underprivileged and the persecuted ...

To me, Christianity is not words but living the gospel out in life. The deeds of daily living in the marketplace must authenticate the words we have heard on a Sunday and offered in worship. We must be doers of the word not hearers only.

*(Canon Brian Lougheed,* The Kerryman, *18 December 1987)*


I believe life is what you make it to be. What you have to watch out for is balance in life. If one doesn't, one can be very unhappy. Because a lot of my life is solitary, I balance this. I really need solitude and I need people. I need both. No one can exist on their own. We all need each other.

*(Maria Simmonds-Gooding, 'Spirit of the Blaskets travels with Maria like a first love',* The Kerryman, *26 June 1998)*


It baffles me to hear people saying they really like playing, but, on the other hand, they bend the rules to achieve success which means victory.

I couldn't do that. Anyway it never crossed my mind to bend the rules.

My father was the biggest influence of my life because what he did was correct. You couldn't bluff your way. That was the ethos I had in living. To take on the challenge.

Success means many things to many people. Some people think victories, trophies and medals are what matter most. To me these things were incidental. I just liked the actual playing, but definitely I was lucky.

*(Mick O'Connell quoted in 'Mick O'Connell, A Football Legend',*
The Kerryman, *18 February 2000)*


I know that doubts may come but they will go just as quick if you can face them down and dismantle them. Accept them, then attack them, break them down into small pieces and leave them on the ground behind you as you walk on to the next challenge. I know that if in doubt, practise. Practice kills all doubt.

*(Paul Galvin,* In My Own Words*)*


'Tis better I'm getting every day. Of course, I'll keep going. Sit down in a chair is it? Anyone who ever sat in a chair failed and just died.

The harder the work is the better I like it. Young lads today know nothing about work and if you try to teach 'em they won't listen to you – maybe one in 20 of 'em might.

*(Eugene (Eugie) O'Sullivan (90), a drover at Kenmare Mart,*
*interviewed by Donal Hickey, 'Mart comes to a halt for legend Eugie',*
The Irish Examiner, *10 February 2015)*

Shíos síos ar phort na trá, mar a raibh radharc álainn i mo thimpeall. Is marbh an croí nach dtógfadh aer bog cumhra na farraige an smúit agus an brón de.

I sat down on the bank above the beach where I had a splendid view all around me. Dead indeed is the heart from which the balmy air of the sea cannot banish sorrow and grief.

*(Peig Sayers,* Peig*)*


Happy is the childhood that has a river flowing through it.

*(Bryan MacMahon,* The Master*)*


People who are ashamed of their addresses should remember that Christ was born in a stable and people who are proud of their addresses should remember it even more.

*(John B. Keane,* The Little Book of John B. Keane*)*


No choice. No say. No matter. It was given to me as easy as dinner. I couldn't believe it, that all I had was 16 years here and soon I began to pay attention to every detail that was going on in this town.

I realised I was fighting for my life for the third time in four years and this time I have to die.

Yet still I hear of young people committing suicide, and I'm sorry but it makes me feel nothing but anger.

I feel angry that these people choose to take their lives, to ruin their families and to leave behind a mess that no one can clean up.

Yet I am here with no choice, trying as best I can to prepare my family and friends for what's about to come and leave as little a mess as possible.

I know that most of these people could be going through financial despair and have other problems in life, but I am at the depths of despair and, believe me, there is a long way to go before you get to where I am.

For these people, no matter how bad life gets, there are no reasons bad enough to make them do this; if they slept on it or looked for help they could find a solution, and they need to think of the consequences of what they are about to do.

So please, as a 16-year-old who has no say in his death sentence, who has no choice in the pain he is about to cause and who would take any chance at even a few more months on this planet, appreciate what you have, know that there are always other options and help is always there.

*(Tralee teenager Donal Walsh (1996–2013), who was awarded a* Kerry's Eye/Radio Kerry Local Hero *award in March 2013, made his first public plea to his peers to reject suicide in an essay published in* Kerry's Eye *as part of an interview with journalist Aidan O'Connor, 27 March 2013. His call subsequently went nationwide through an appearance on 'The Brendan O'Connor Show' and a further essay in* The Sunday Independent*)*

While today Donal is known for his stance on suicide, it is important to remember Donal died from one of the biggest modern-day killers. Cancer. While suffering this disease, Donal was an ambassador for cancer awareness and advocated at national and international level, even to the United Nations, to increase research and funding into this killer disease. If he was alive today, he would be the first one to support me in asking the upcoming G8 summit to increase funding and advance possible cures for cancer.

*(Extract from eulogy of Donal's mother, Elma, at his funeral. Fionnbar Walsh,* Donal's Mountain: How One Son Inspired a Nation*)*

How wise to have believed that the world is richer than the economic eye allows it to be.

*(John Moriarty,* Nostos*)*

A wise man once told me, 'Many of the woes of mankind arise from these three insecurities: insecure gentility, insecure scholarship, insecure authority.'

*(Bryan MacMahon,* The Master*)*

# FAMINE

The fields appear as if fire had passed over them.

*(Thomas de Moleyns writing from Dublin to the Relief Commission, gives a graphic description of the devastation caused by the total potato crop failure of 1846)*


Whole families used to starve in their cabins without their plight being discovered until the stench of their decaying corpses attracted notice.

*(Samuel Hussey,* The Reminiscences of an Irish Land Agent*)*


The potato crop in Kerry is ruined, and we urgently advise that the government be at once called on to provide food for the people.

*(*Kerry Examiner, *2 August 1846)*


I have written to you in former letters about miserable hovels in other parts of Ireland; they are more than equalled in Kerry. I have described the half-naked and potato-fed people I have met with elsewhere, here their nakedness is not less and they know no other food. In filthiness and squalid poverty, starving on a rood of land with miles of waste land around him, which the application of industry and knowledge would make teem with plenty, the poor Kerry farmer exists in contented wretchedness.

*(T. C. Foster's observations on Kerry's poor, in* Letters on the Condition of the People of Ireland*)*


I have received last evening your circular announcing a meeting to be held this day in the court-house, for the purpose of entering into arrangements to procure food for our famishing people. I should, if able, most cheerfully attend, but have not as yet fully recovered from the effects of a very painful and tedious gout – and knowing that in some cases there must be gratuitous distribution, I should on this as on all former occasions, contribute my mite, and feel it due to public opinion, to explain why at this time I am not a contributor. My means, though limited, are more than sufficient to answer my ordinary demands, but for the last three years I am engaged in the construction of a public building that cost me over £3,000 more than the subscriptions to it, and consequently am not only drained of every shilling I could call my own, but am burdened with a weighty debt.

*(Bishop Cornelius Egan writing to the secretary of the Killarney Relief Committee, 25 March 1846.* Kerry Examiner, *31 March 1846)*

On Friday last, thirty horses which had been sent to Cork for Indian meal, were detained on the road near Glenflesk by the frost. Nothing could describe the consternation – the panic which seized upon the people of Kenmare.

*(Rev. John O'Sullivan, Kenmare's parish priest, 16 December 1846, in T. C. Foster's* Letters on the Condition of the People of Ireland*)*


Only for the position in which I am placed as a clergyman I would quit the country and turn to some other profession.

*(Rev. John O'Sullivan reacting to the worsening situation in Kenmare, 16 December 1846, in T. C. Foster's* Letters on the Condition of the People of Ireland*)*


I daily witness the most terrible spectacles. Men and women are discoloured with dropsy, attacked with dysentery or mad with fever on the works – driven there by the terrible necessity of trying to get as much as would purchase a meal … With most of these, working is a mockery, they can scarcely walk to and from the roads, and how can they work? Better by far to keep them in their wretched hovels and paying them for staying there, than to ask them to expose themselves for a day on the side of a mountain.

*(Thomas Gill, Board of Works inspecting officer, in a letter to the prime minister, 25 February 1847,* Correspondence, January–March 1847, Board of Works*)*

If ever a government deserves to be damned in public estimation the present one does, for the mode it adopted for supplying the country with food.

(Kerry Examiner, *2 October 1846*)

In Russia, the proprietors of large estates worked by slaves, are obliged to feed and clothe their slaves. In Ireland, it quite depends on the will of the proprietor whether he will let his lands to his tenants, which will enable them to feed their families on the coarsest food, and to clothe them in the coarsest raiment. If a famine occurs – and in some parts of Ireland famines are of annual occurrence – the landlord is not obliged to do anything for his tenant, but the tenant must pay his rent …

The people were almost starving. They could scarcely get a sufficiency of the poorest food, yet they were compelled to pay rent and tithes far above the value of their land. If they were unable to pay, they were put out upon the wayside to die like dogs …

(*Sister Mary Francis Clare (1829–99), born Margaret Anna Cusack and known as the Nun of Kenmare, in Irene ffrench Eagar's* The Nun of Kenmare)

It was no small achievement in 1879 or 1880 to collect £15,000 (worth about £250,000 today) for a Famine Relief

Fund. The money poured in, in response to her cleverly-worded, appealing letters published in a variety of newspapers and journals, particularly those whose editors or owners had Irish sympathies such as Galway-born Patrick Ford's *Irish World* in New York. In many cases the money was sent directly to the Convent at Kenmare and merely addressed to 'The Nun of Kenmare' – the shadowy figure who had become a symbol of liberation.

*(Irene ffrench Eagar,* The Nun of Kenmare*)*


… a magnificent building, a strange contrast to the misery, dirt and wretchedness around.

*(Sister Mary Francis Clare describes Saint Mary's Cathedral, Killarney, which was built during the Famine of the 1840s, in Irene ffrench Eagar's* The Nun of Kenmare*)*


It was the misfortune of this country that an imbecile minister and a shamefully weak and corrupt government came into office.

*(Dr McEnery, parish priest of Tralee, speaking from the altar, 9 January 1847, in T. C. Foster's* Letters on the Condition of the People of Ireland*)*


A poor woman and her three children left Dingle for Tralee, to seek relief in the workhouse when every other source had failed. Faintness from want of food overcame the wretched creature, and she had to lie down. In a short time a passer-by found this hapless group – the mother dead and the children whom she must have starved herself to feed, crying over the remains of their parent.

*(*Kerry Evening Post*, 19 December 1846)*

This neighbourhood is becoming depopulated at railway speed. I see nothing within the bounds of possibility that can save the people. On one road, on which I have 300 men employed, the deaths are three each day. This is in the parish of Tuosist. The people are buried without coffins, frequently in the next field. No noise or sign of grief for the dead: every thought is selfish and unfeeling. No man looks beyond tomorrow, or to any but himself, every person seems jealous and suspicious of his fellow.

*(Thomas Gill, Board of Works inspecting officer, in a letter to the prime minister, 25 February 1847,* Correspondence, January–March 1847, Board of Works*)*

Though my Aunt Bridgie was old she didn't remember the great famine but as a child she had heard older people talk about it. She described a house to us where distant relations of our own lived in Glounacoppal. The family lay on the kitchen floor too far gone from hunger to stand up. The father and mother had watched the younger children die one by one. He decided he would try again to find some sustenance for his wife and only surviving son. A raw turnip, maybe half-hidden and forgotten in the garden, or dandelion roots which he could dig up with his fingers. He crawled out of the house and was later found dead in a field clutching a bunch of dandelion roots in his hand.

*(Éamon Kelly,* The Apprentice*)*


So bad was the famine that people coming in from the country fell in the street never to rise again. One woman was found lying on the outskirts of the town almost dead from starvation, her three children having succumbed beside her, and had she not been carried to the soup kitchen she would not have survived them many hours …

My wife well remembers another case. One day her mother emerged from a cabin carrying what looked like a big bundle of clothes. It was the form of an emaciated woman, whose four children and husband had all starved. My mother-in-law took her to her own house, fed her at first with spoonfuls of soup, and kept her there until she had rebuilt her once vigorous constitution.

My wife subsequently recollects her as a hale, buxom, young widow coming to say goodbye before emigrating to America.

*(Samuel Hussey,* The Reminiscences of an Irish Land Agent*)*

*Daniel O'Connell on the famine:*

Take immediate precautions for the Derrynane district [to prevent spread of cholera]. Get a cow or two killed, one after the other, and distributed in broth and beef among the poorest classes of my tenants. It is the best precaution. Totally stop the sale of whiskey ... send 2 or 3 gallons of pure brandy to Derrynane [medicinal].

*(Letter to John Primrose from London, March 1834, in Maurice R. O'Connell (ed.),* The Correspondence of Daniel O'Connell*)*

As far as I am concerned, spare no expense that can possibly alleviate the sufferings of the people ... Everybody should live as full as possible, eating meat twice a day. Get meat for the poor as much as possible ... before all things, be prodigal of relief out of my means – beef, bread, mutton, medicines, physician, everything you can think of.

*(Letter to John Primrose from London, March 1834, in Maurice R. O'Connell (ed.),* The Correspondence of Daniel O'Connell*)*

I wish you to be as abundant to the people as you possibly can, recollecting however that we have dreadful times before us.

*(Letter to his son, Maurice, December 1846)*

Ireland is in your hands and in your power. If you do not save her, she cannot save herself. And I solemnly call on you to bear in mind what I am telling you now in advance, something of which I am absolutely certain, that one out of every four of her people will soon die unless you come to her aid.

*(Daniel O'Connell, pleading for aid for famine victims, in his last speech in the House of Commons on 8 February 1847, Hansard)*

# PRAYERS, BLESSINGS, CURSES

May your hand kill a pig.

>*(Maidhc Dainín Ó Sé*, House Don't Fall on Me*)*

That you may rear a bishop.

>*(Unknown)*

Grant me a sense of humour, Lord,
The saving grace to see a joke,
To win some humour out of life,
And pass it on to other folk.

>*(Verse seen by me on a souvenir plaque in the window of O'Neill's Shop, Henn Street, in the 1960s as I made my way to school)*

May the Lord above
Send down a dove,
With wings as sharp as razors
To cut the hide of Paddy Thaidhg
For serving all his neighbours.

>*(Joe Dineen criticising Paddy Thaidhg, one of Lord Kenmare's bailiffs*, Journal of Cumann Luachra, *November 1983)*

God has no country.

> *(Epitaph on the grave of Monsignor Hugh O'Flaherty in the grounds of the Daniel O'Connell Memorial Church, Cahersiveen)*

She prayed for the lonely traveller, for the sailor tossed by the tempest, for our emigrants, for the poor souls, for the sinner who was at that very moment standing before the judgement seat of God and last of all for all of her family:

*God bless and save us all,*
*St Patrick, Bridget and Colmcille guard each wall,*
*May the Queen of Heaven and angels bright*
*Keep us and our home from all harm this night!*

> *(Éamon Kelly,* The Apprentice*)*

Glory to God in the highest, and on earth, peace, good will to men.

> *(The first message sent via the transatlantic cable on 16 August 1858 between Valentia Harbour in Ireland and Trinity Bay in Newfoundland)*

May no gale of wind ever pass by your backside, but may they all take the shortcut in.

> *(Brenda Ní Shúilleabháin's* Bibeanna: Memories from a Corner of Ireland*)*

St Brigid, Mary of Ireland, cover us with your cloak,
St Brigid, generous heart, direct us on the right path.
St Brigid, graceful, loving, protect us from our enemies,
St Brigid, beautiful nun at the hour of our death, call us to you.

*('Prayer for St Brigid', Anecdotes, in Brenda Ní Shúilleabháin's*
Bibeanna: Memories from a Corner of Ireland*)*

May the snails devour his corpse,
And the rains do harm worse;
May the devil sweep the hairy creature soon;

*(Carthalawn in John B. Keane's* Sive*)*

'God's curse on you, Red Ellie,' he cried. 'May the flagstones of hell blister your heels for eternity.'

*(Sigerson Clifford, 'The Red-Haired Woman',
in* Irish Short Stories*)*

I happen to know that God's greatest blessing is a good housekeeper but that God's greatest curse is a bad one.

*(Father Best in* Moll *by John B. Keane)*

# SCHOOLING

For a school is nothing if not a place of laughter and song.

*(Bryan MacMahon,* The Master*)*


We all walked to school barefooted all year round. As soon as the month of October came, all of us had to take 2 sods of turf to heat the school. The only one who got near that fire was the teacher.

*(Pádraig Mac Giolla Phádraig, 'The Days of My Youth',
in Finbarr Bracken's* Ballinskelligs Remembered*)*


He [Master Fleming] had beehives by the hedge there. It was our duty to come out with him and inspect the hives. Not every one of the students was a saint. They would deliberately tease the bees and we had to fly in all directions.

He was a remarkable teacher. He taught us gardening. He taught me my first Latin. He taught Greek and he was very interested in the derivation of words. He wrote a book on Kilcummin family names with John Lyne.

*(Michael O'Connor, 'Post Office offers a window on the past',*
The Kerryman, *25 August 1995)*

If you ever travel on the mountain road that leads from the south to the magic land of Lyreacrompane, you will pass by a lonely sight – a building that was once a national school.

I spent a few months there as deputy for a neighbour who was on maternity leave and learned more from my pupils than they did from me.

They ranged from about five years of age to about ten; there were days when I loved them one and all – and days when I wished The Pied Piper of Hamelin would come back and lead them all down to the swift waters of The Smearla.

Mountain children are lightning on the verbal draw: you would have a better chance of winning a duel with a Moore Street trader.

On my first day I said to an offender, 'I'll kill you.' And he said: 'If you kill me sir, you'll have to bury me.' ... Patrick Kavanagh's magic tribute to his mother was a great favourite: one afternoon I asked my little scholars why they liked it – and a wee lass put up a hand, her own, and said: 'Because it's about our own kind of life.'

*(Con Houlihan, 'Renagown NS – higher education in a magic land',*
*in* Windfalls*)*


The greatest intellectual disadvantage that anyone can carry through life is the inability to read.

*(Bryan MacMahon,* The Master*)*

## Schooling

The grown boys played football in the little field attached to the school. The ball was made of long cloth strips, wound solidly and hand-sewn with every conceivable kind of twine. It had a certain amount of dull bounce, and it made do.

*(Michael Kirby, Skelligside)*


I thank the goodness and the grace,
Which on my birth has smiled
And me in these Christian times,
A happy English child.

*(This poem was recited every morning in North Kerry's Slieveadara National School in North Kerry which opened in 1843. Bertie O'Connor-Kerry, 'Slieveadara School: 150 Years of Education',* Ballyduff Magazine, *1994)*


Speaking about an old schoolmaster, someone once said to me that a good teacher leaves the print of his teeth on a parish for three generations. I realised that each child had a gift, and that the 'leading out' of that gift was the proper goal of teaching. To me a great teacher was simply a great person teaching.

*(Bryan MacMahon, The Master)*


I learned the grammar of four dead languages – Irish, English, Latin and Greek – in St Michael's. I did Maths and things like that and knew as much as anyone about fractions and so I was perceived to be educated.

> *(John Moriarty in Micheál Ó Muircheartaigh's*
> From Borroloola to Mangerton Mountain*)*

Perhaps the biggest wrench in life is going to school. It may not seem so very much afterwards – as the boy said of the tooth when he looked at it in the dentist's forceps – but the wrench is really bad.

I learned my letters from my mother, and picked up a few other smatterings before I had daily lessons from a tutor at Dingle. Strange to say, a very good classical education could have been obtained there in the thirties [1830s], better, so far as I can estimate, than could have been expected from a town double the size at the same period in England.

> *(Samuel Hussey,* The Reminiscences of an Irish Land Agent*)*

Education is part of a person's life, that's for the young generation. The older generation they didn't go to school that much but they knew more than the ones that were at school because they learned themselves. My father's mother and father died when he was very young and he looked after his three brothers making buckets and gallons, he had to do for himself and the rest of them. He knew more than if he'd been going to school all his life. He went to school for a few months to make his confirmation and then out and back to do his own schooling.

*(Unidentified participant in Kerry Travellers' Development Project, Do you no mydell?)*


If the Roman Catholics of England send their sons to Oxford and Cambridge, why should not more Irish Roman Catholics send theirs to Trinity College, Dublin? Only a very few do, although the education is said to be quite as good as either of the great English Universities. A far tighter hold is kept, however, on the Roman Catholic laity in Ireland than in England. It always surprises English people to learn that, in Ireland, Roman Catholics are not allowed to enter Protestant churches to attend either funerals or weddings. Nor do I think there is much probability of these restrictions being removed.

*(Samuel Hussey,* The Reminiscences of an Irish Land Agent*)*


It was the terror. The terror of everyone, the entire town, my parents, watching me fail … I learned all I know from that experience. Everything.

*(Michael Fassbender referring to a teenage adaptation of Quentin Tarantino's 'Reservoir Dogs' in Revelles Night Club, Killarney, in which he played Mr Pink and a lamb chop was used for a 'cop's severed ear'. Interview by Jonathan Heaf,* GQ.co.uk*)*

I did not fully understand then that many of the students came from small farms, and were well fed and clad, but many more were the children of the poor ... There was buttered bread and bottles of milk in the satchels of the fortunate. The poor dipped their fingers in their pockets to feel for their unbuttered slices and ate the dry morsels.

*(Rory O'Connor,* Gander at the Gate*)*


As a youngster, Jerry Fleming from Killarney was locked out of the world of books because he couldn't read. Despite his literacy problems, he had a real passion for books and would have given anything to join the old library in the Town Hall.

'I used to go down there and stand in the hall and smell the books,' he said. 'Kitty used to come out and try to get me to come in but I'd run away.'

The librarian, Kitty O'Connor, subsequently became a great friend of Jerry's and encouraged him never to give up on his dream to learn to read ...

'I remember one Christmas my mother was going through the Santa list and I wanted *Treasure Island*,' he said. 'She asked me why did I want it when I couldn't read.'

'I got it anyway and I used to keep it under my pillow,' he said. 'I could almost invent the story for myself when I looked at the cover' ...

Taking his courage in his hands (as an adult), he enrolled with the Kerry Education and Training Board for the Intensive Tuition in Basic Adult Education Programme, held in Killarney ...

'The important thing is not to be afraid to make a mistake,' he said. 'I'd recommend to anybody with time on their hands to go back into education.'

*('Reading reveals new world for Jerry',*
Kerry's Eye, *4 January 2014)*

# BIBLIOGRAPHY

Beatty, Bertha, *Kerry Memories* (The Channing Press, Devon, England, 1939, and North Kerry Literary Trust, Listowel, County Kerry, 2007)

Berney, K. A. (ed.), *Contemporary British Dramatists* (Gale, 1994)

Bracken, Finbarr, *Ballinskelligs Remembered* (Coiste Forbartha na Sceilge, 2014)

Brennan, Fiona, *George Fitzmaurice: 'Wild in His Own Way'. Biography of an Abbey Playwright* (Carysfort Press, 2005)

Clemenger, Michael, *Holy Terrors. A Boy. Two Brothers. A Stolen Childhood* (The O'Brien Press, 2009)

Clifford, Sigerson, *Irish Short Stories* (Mercier Press, 1989)

Collins, Stephen, *Spring and the Labour Story* (The O'Brien Press, 1993)

Corridan, Michael, 'Remembering Maura Moriarty', *Caherdaniel Parish Magazine*, 2015

Crowley, John, and Sheehan, John (eds), *The Iveragh Peninsula: A Cultural Atlas of the Ring of Kerry* (Cork University Press, 2009)

Curran, John, *Just My Luck* (self-published, 1993)

Daunt, William J. O'Neill, *Personal Recollections of the Late Daniel O'Connell, MP, 1775–1847* (Chapman & Hall, 1848)

Deenihan, Jimmy, *My Sporting Life* (Red Hen Publishing, 2011)

de Faoite, Seamus, *The More We Are Together* (Poolbeg Press, 1980)

de Moleyns, Thomas, Letter to the Relief Commission (National

Archives, Relief Commission Incoming Letters: Numerical Sub-Series: Kerry, RLFC3/1/5592)

Donovan, Katie, Jeffares, A. Norman and Kennelly, Brendan (eds), *Ireland's Women: Writings Past and Present* (Gill and Macmillan, 1994)

Eagar, Irene ffrench, *The Nun of Kenmare* (Mercier Press, 1970)

Erde, Maureen, *Help! I'm an Irish Innkeeper* (Poolbeg, 1997)

Ferguson, Catherine, *Margaret Anna Cusack (The Nun of Kenmare): Knock, November 1881–December 1883* (GaelBooks, 2008)

Fitzmaurice, Gabriel, *Kerry Through Its Writers* (New Island Books, 1993)

— *The Kerry Anthology* (Marino Books, 2000)

Fitzmaurice, George, 'The Magic Glasses' in *The Plays of George Fitzmaurice: Dramatic Fantasies*, edited by Austin Clarke (The Dolmen Press, 1967)

Fleming, Brian, *The Vatican Pimpernel: The Wartime Exploits of Monsignor Hugh O'Flaherty* (Collins Press, 2014)

Flower, Robin, *The Western Island* (Clarendon Press, 1944)

Fogarty, Weeshie, *Dr Eamonn O'Sullivan: A Man Before His Time* (Merlin Publishing, 2007)

Foster, T. C., *Letters on the Condition of the People of Ireland* (Chapman & Hall, 1846)

Galvin, Paul, *In My Own Words: The Autobiography* (Transworld Ireland, 2014)

Gordon, Hal, 'Irish Bull', www.punditwire.com

Hannon, Katie, *The Naked Politician: Your Local TD will Never seem Quite the Same Again* (Gill & Macmillan, 2004)

Hayward, Richard, *In the Kingdom of Kerry* (W. Tempest, Dundalgan Press, 1976)

Heaf, Jonathan, 'Michael Fassbender: Evil never looked this good', www.gq-magazine.co.uk/entertainment/articles/2013-12/28/michael-fassbender-cover-photos-interview, 3 February 2014

Hickey, Donal, *The Mighty Healy-Rae: A Biography* (Marino Books, 1997)

Houlihan, Con, *More Than a Game* (Liberties Press, 2003)

— *Windfalls* (Boglark Press, 1996)

— *In So Many Words: The Best of Con Houlihan* (Mercier Press, 2002)

Humphries, Tom, *Green Fields* (Orion Publishing, 1996)

Hussey, Samuel, *The Reminiscences of an Irish Land Agent* (Duckworth & Co., 1904)

Joy, Breda, *Hidden Kerry: The Keys to the Kingdom* (Mercier Press, 2014)

Keane, Fergal, *All of These People: A Memoir* (HarperCollins, 2005)

Keane, John B., *Many Young Men of Twenty* (Progress House, 1961)

— *Unlawful Sex and Other Testy Matters* (Mercier Press, 1978)

— *Three Plays: Sive, The Field, Big Maggie* (Mercier Press, 1990)

— *Moll* (Mercier Press, 1991)

— *The Year of the Hiker* (Mercier Press, 1991)

— *Celebrated Letters of John B. Keane*, Vol. 1 (Mercier Press, 1997)

— *The Little Book of John B. Keane* (Mercier Press, 2000)

Keane, Moss, with Billy Keane, *Rucks, Mauls & Gaelic Football* (Merlin Publishing, 2005)

Keenan, Donal, *Páidí: A Big Life* (Hero Books, 2013)

Kelly, Éamon, *In My Father's Time: An Evening of Storytelling* (Mercier Press, 1976)

— *The Apprentice* (Marino Books, 1995)

— *Ireland's Master Storyteller: The Collected Stories of Éamon Kelly* (Marino Books, 1998)

Kerry Travellers' Development Project, *Do you no mydell? Poems, Stories & Pictures by Travellers in Kerry* (2002)

Kirby, Michael, *Skelligside* (The Lilliput Press, 1990)

MacMahon, Bryan, *The Master* (Poolbeg, 1992)

Maguire, Pauline, *The Last Move* (Maguire Family Archive, unpublished manuscript, 1955)

— *Green Dust* (Maguire Family Archive, unpublished manuscript, 1955)

Maxwell, Constantia, *The Stranger in Ireland from the Reign of Elizabeth to the Great Famine* (Jonathan Cape, 1954)

McAuliffe, Dr Mary, 'Cumann na mBan in Kerry', public lecture delivered in Listowel, 17 April 2014

McCarthy, Pete, *McCarthy's Bar: A Journey of Discovery in Ireland* (Hodder and Stoughton, 2000)

McCrohan, Owen, *Mick O'Dwyer: The Authorised Biography* (Kerry Mod Publications, 1990)

Moriarty, John, *Turtle was Gone a Long Time. Vol. 1: Crossing the Kedron* (The Lilliput Press, 1997)

— *Nostos* (The Lilliput Press, 2011)

Morton, H. V., *In Search of Ireland* (Methuen London Ltd, 1980)

Murphy, Annie, with Peter de Rosa, *Forbidden Fruit: The True Story of My Secret Love for Eamonn Casey, the Bishop of Galway* (Little, Brown and Company, 1993)

Murphy, Jeremiah, *When Youth Was Mine: A Memoir of Kerry 1902–1925* (Mentor Press, 1998)

Neville, Grace, 'Daniel O'Connell: Food, Feast and Famine', paper delivered at the Daniel O'Connell Summer School in Cahersiveen on 29 August 2014

Ní Shúilleabháin, Brenda (ed.), *Bibeanna: Memories from a Corner of Ireland* (Mercier Press, 2007)

Ó Criomhthain, Tomás, *An tOileánach*, eag. Pádraig Ua Maoileoin (Helicon Teoranta, 1980)

Ó Luing, Seán, *I Die in a Good Cause: A Study of Thomas Ashe, Idealist and Revolutionary* (Anvil Books, 1970)

Ó Mathúna, Seán, 'Marriage Sliabh Luachra Style', *Journal of Cumann Luachra*, Vol. 1, No. 2, November 1983

Ó Muircheartaigh, Micheál, *From Borroloola to Mangerton Mountain: Travels and Stories from Ireland's Most Beloved Broadcaster, Micheál Ó Muircheartaigh* (Penguin Ireland, 2006)

Ó Sé, Maidhc Dainín, *House Don't Fall on Me* (translated by Gabriel Fitzmaurice, Mercier Press, 2007)

O'Connell, Eugene, (ed.), *Cork Literary Review*, Vol. XV (Bradshaw Books, 2013)

O'Connell, Maurice R. (ed.), *The Correspondence of Daniel O'Connell*, Vol. I (1792–1814) (Irish University Press for the Irish Manuscripts Commission, 1972)

— *The Correspondence of Daniel O'Connell*, Vol. V (1833–1836) (Irish Manuscripts Commission, 1977)

O'Connor, Jack, *The Keys to the Kingdom* (Penguin Ireland, 2007)

O'Connor, Joseph, *Hostage to Fortune* (Michael F. Moynihan Publishing Company, 1955)

O'Connor, Rory, *Gander at the Gate* (The Lilliput Press, 2000)

O'Connor-Kerry, Bertie, 'Slieveadara School: 150 years of official education', *Ballyduff Magazine*, 1994

O'Leary, John, *On the Doorsteps: Memoirs of a Long-serving TD* (Irish Political Memoirs, 2015)

O'Shea, Owen, *Heirs to the Kingdom: Kerry's Political Dynasties* (The O'Brien Press, 2011)

O'Sullivan, Maurice, *Twenty Years A-Growing* (reprint, Oxford University Press, 2000)

O'Sullivan, Valerie, *I am of Kerry* (Currach Press, 2003)

Quill, Shirley, *Michael Quill, Himself: A Memoir* (Devin-Adair, 1985)

Sayers, Peig, *An Old Woman's Reflections* (Oxford University Press, 1978)

— *Peig: The Autobiography of Peig Sayers of the Great Blasket Island* (Edco, 1999)

Smith, Charles, *The Ancient and Present State of the County of Kerry* (reprint, Mercier Press, 1969)

Synge, J. M., *John M. Synge in West Kerry* (Mercier Press, 1979)

Walsh, Fionnbar (written with June Considine), *Donal's Mountain: How One Son Inspired a Nation* (Hachette Books, 2014)

Woulfe, Jimmy, *Voices of Kerry: Conversations with Men and Women of Kerry* (Blackwater Press, 1994)

## ALSO BY THIS AUTHOR

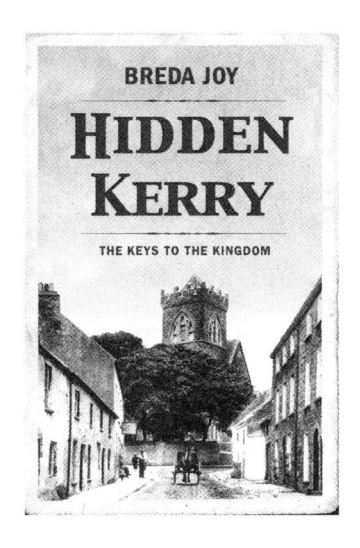

**BREDA JOY**
# HIDDEN KERRY
THE KEYS TO THE KINGDOM

*Hidden Kerry* takes you on the less-travelled paths of the Kingdom. The journey begins at Tarbert on the River Shannon and finishes close to the Cork border under the Paps Mountains. Lose yourself in the story of Lord Kenmare's forgotten mansion, which hosted royal visits until it was consumed by fire; the daring plot hatched in Dingle to rescue Marie Antoinette; and the tale of the German U-boat that landed Greek sailors at Ventry in the Second World War. Meet vibrant characters such as Mrs Elizabeth Herbert, who threw up her life in Muckross House to run away with her lover; and Fr Francis O'Sullivan, a gun-running friar who was beheaded on Scariff Island by Cromwellian soldiers. A book that is as much for the locals as it is for the visitors, *Hidden Kerry* takes you off the beaten track and brings the Kingdom to life.

*www.mercierpress.ie*

# MERCIER PRESS
## Irish Publisher - Irish Story

We hope you enjoyed this book.

Since 1944, Mercier Press has published books that have been critically important to Irish life and culture.

Our website is the best place to find out more information about Mercier, our books, authors, news and the best deals on a wide variety of books. Mercier tracks the best prices for our books online and we seek to offer the best value to our customers, offering free delivery within Ireland.

A large selection of Mercier's new releases and backlist are also available as ebooks. We have an ebook for everyone, with titles available for the Amazon Kindle, Sony Reader, Kobo Reader, Apple products and many more. Visit our website to find and buy our ebooks.

Sign up on our website or complete and return the form below to receive updates and special offers.

www.mercierpress.ie
www.facebook.com/mercier.press
www.twitter.com/irishpublisher

---

Name: _____
Email: _____
Address: _____
Mobile No.: _____

Mercier Press, Unit 3b, Oak House, Bessboro Rd, Blackrock, Cork, Ireland